PSYCHOPHYSIOLOGICAL MEASUREMENT OF COVERT BEHAVIOR:

A Guide for the Laboratory

PSYCHOPHYSIOLOGICAL MEASUREMENT OF COVERT BEHAVIOR:

A Guide for the Laboratory

F. J. McGUIGAN
University of Louisville

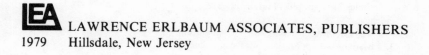

LAWRENCE ERLBAUM ASSOCIATES, PUBLISHERS
1979   Hillsdale, New Jersey

DISTRIBUTED BY THE HALSTED PRESS DIVISION OF
JOHN WILEY & SONS
New York   Toronto   London   Sydney

Lawrence Erlbaum Associates, Inc., Publishers
365 Broadway
Hillsdale, New Jersey 07642

Distributed solely by Halsted Press Division
John Wiley & Sons, Inc., New York

Library of Congress Cataloging in Publication Data
McGuigan, Frank J.
 Psychophysiological measurement of covert
behavior.

 Includes bibliographical references and
indexes.
  1. Psychology, Physiological. 2. Cognition.
3. Physiological apparatus. 4. Psychological
apparatus. I. Title. [DNLM: 1. Psychophysiology—Laboratory manuals. WL25 M145p]
QP360.M33   152   79-18482
ISBN 0-470-26814-X

Printed in the United States of America

Dedicated to my good colleagues and dear friends:
John R. Everett
W. Horsley Gantt
Edna Grubb
Donald J. Lewis
Meredith Richards
Ralph Steinhart
Howard Thorsheim
Ronald Webster
Lowell Wine
Endre Szirmai

CONTENTS

Psychology has made sizable advances with its primary emphasis on the study of overt behavior, but its progress on covert behavior has been retarded because of the lack of suitable psychophysiological technology. This work was written to help laboratory researchers in their efforts to develop a mature science of covert behavior. Early efforts to record small-scale behavior with flattened wine glasses about the tongue were heroic, but, understandably, progress did not begin until the recent advent of very sensitive electronic equipment. We are now technologically capable of: (1) sensing; (2) amplifying; (3) recording; and (4) quantifying small-scale behavior with at least the effectiveness with which we have studied large-scale responses. It is hoped that this book will facilitate the empirical efforts of future psychophysiologists (advanced undergraduate and graduate students) and professional researchers in each of these four phases of the laboratory system. This book also may be useful in lecture and laboratory courses in psychophysiology and physiological psychology, and it may find a place in relevant research laboratories.

More generally, this book hopefully will serve as an important component in our overall efforts to understand behavior. Elsewhere, we have attempted to summarize the existing empirical basis for cognitive psychophysiology in the areas of covert eye behavior, covert oral and nonoral responses, and electrical measures of neurophysiological activity (McGuigan, 1978). There we also attempted to provide a theoretical framework for such covert psychophysiological processes. Psychophysiology has developed almost exclusively as an empirical science with little guiding theory; conversely, psychology has developed by means of an $S-(X)-R$ mediational paradigm such that covert processes (X) have only been hypothesized and indirectly inferred from antecedent S and consequent R events. Our strategy has been to wed the empiricism of laboratory psychophysiology with the mediational paradigm of behaviorism such that these approaches become mutually facilitative. The direct measurement of hypothetical constructs through electromyography and electroencephalography makes for progress in the traditional psychological approach. Similarly, psychophysiology benefits from a guiding theoretical framework furnished by psychology. Hopefully, the present effort will contribute to this cross fertilization.

There have been several works in the past that contributed well to these purposes, such as J. F. Davis' (1959) classical laboratory manual, but none individually or collectively accomplished what is attempted here, because they offer only fractionated information, are dated, or are not readily available. Hopefully, then, this effort is a unique one.

Among those to whom I express my special appreciation are the psychophysiologists who pioneered our field, especially Hans Berger, R. C. Davis, Edmund Jacobson, Luther Mays, and my students who over the years have labored so diligently for long hours with me in the laboratory, where we discovered many of these items of information. I should single out Brad Davis for assisting with the figures herein and for his contributions to our work in cognitive psychophysiology in many respects.

F. J. McGUIGAN

PSYCHOPHYSIOLOGICAL MEASUREMENT OF COVERT BEHAVIOR:
A Guide for the Laboratory

OVERVIEW OF PSYCHOPHYSIOLOGY

Psychophysiology is a broad field in which there are attempts to accomplish many purposes. Some purposes have to do strictly with functioning of organs and systems within the body, neighboring on physiology. Others stand closer to those of psychology, having to do more with bodily response systems during cognitive functioning.[1] Psychophysiology is thus an interdisciplinary field encompassing many aspects of physiology and psychology. Psychophysiologists may therefore have been trained in such areas as physiology, psychology, medicine, and engineering. The methods developed, and to be discussed here, should be generally applicable to psychophysiological problems regardless of specific purposes—the electromyographer, for instance, could equally well study large scale movements of the limb within the context of exercise physiology or the small-scale movements of the tongue during silent reading. Our emphases will be primarily on those problems concerning cognitive functioning, the traditional goal of psychology.

In addressing the question of the nature of the human mind, contemporary psychologists are busily engaged in efforts to directly measure the higher mental processes with psychophysiological techniques. In considering the question of where in the body thoughts occur, an objective scientist would eschew any predisposing biases, considering it possible that any or all bodily systems might serve some

---

[1]There are few definitions of fields that are commonly accepted and generally adhered to. Psychophysiology is no exception. Three definitions frequently used are: (1) "Any research in which the dependent variable is a physiological measure and the independent variable a 'behavioral' one should be considered psychophysiological research. Thus a distinction between psychophysiology and physiological psychology becomes immediately apparent. The latter deals with the manipulation of physiological variables and the recording of behavioral events while psychophysiology deals with the manipulation of behavioral events and the recording of physiological variables [Stern, 1964, p. 90]." (2) "Psychophysiology is a research area which extends observation of behavior to those covert proceedings of the organism relevant to a psychic state or process under investigation and which can be measured with minimal disturbance to the natural functions involved [Ax, 1964, p. 1]." (3) "Psychophysiology is the science which concerns the physiological activities which underlie or relate to psychic functions [Darrow, 1964, p. 4]."

cognitive function. In fact, research has indicated that most bodily systems are active in cognitive activities. Excellent accounts of brain functioning during thought may be found in Delafresnaye (1954), Eccles (1966), and Young (1970). The eye apparently performs important functions during all types of cognitive acts; Hebb (1968), for instance, held that peripheral activity, especially eye movement, is essential during the formation of images. Chase (1973) offered a general treatment of visual system functioning during various mental acts. Visceral activity has been empirically and theoretically implicated in cognitive processes in a variety of ways. Theoretically, Watson (1930) defined emotion as visceral responding. Interesting empirical work includes that on the esophagus (e.g., Jacobson, 1925), on intestinal activity (e.g., Davis, Garafolo, & Gault, 1957), on electrodermal responding (e.g., Grings 1973a, b), and on the autonomic system in general (e.g., Lacey, 1950; Lacey & Lacey, 1974). Finally, we note that the skeletal musculature has long been held to be covertly active during thought processes (cf. Langfeld, 1933, and M. O. Smith, 1969). The importance of cognitive motor responding was particularly emphasized in Russia and the United States since the latter part of the 19th century. It was Sechenov (1863/1965) who was responsible for initiating a long line of cognitive psychophysiological theorizing and empirical research in Russia. Sechenov's emphasis was on reflexes, and responses, as in his doctrine that "all the endless diversity of the external manifestations of the activity of the brain can be finally regarded as one phenomenon—that of muscular movement [1965, p. 309]." The work of Bechterev (1923), Galperin (1969), Leontiev (1959), Pavlov (e.g., 1941), and Vigotsky (1962) carried Sechenov's reasoning into contemporary Soviet psychology.

In the United States, Titchener (1909) emphasized the role of the skeletal musculature for the development of meaning in his context theory of meaning, though it was the early behaviorists who were primarily responsible for inclining psychology toward our present concentration on the skeletal musculature. Among the early workers in the behavioristic tradition who emphasized the role of the skeletal musculature in the higher mental processes were Dunlap (1912), Holt (1937), Hunter (1924), Langfeld (1931), and Watson (1914). In the early 1930s, Jacobson (1932) greatly advanced the concept of neuromuscular functioning as an explication of cognitive activities.

Recognizing, then, that numerous bodily events may occur during thought, the psychophysiologist has developed a variety of methods for observing and studying those processes. Psychophysiological techniques have been astutely applied in the measurement of covert events in our study of internal information-processing systems during what have been traditionally called *mental processes*. We have found that during any cognitive state the entire body is extremely active. Directly in contrast with the common-sense notion that "the mind shuts down at night during sleep," there is intricate and vigorous interaction of numerous bodily systems; and while silently awake, rather than the common-sense exclamation that "I'm not doing anything, I'm just thinking," the body is also covertly functioning at a very active level.

2
OVERT AND COVERT BEHAVIOR CONTRASTED

The goal of psychology is to understand behavior, and the science has developed with primary emphasis on overt behavior. Psychologists have been impressive in their development of a psychology of overt behavior with the paradigm of relationships between overt response patterns and external environmental events. Although there was some noticeable theorizing about covert behavior in the early part of the century, the technology for studying small-scale responses was simply not available. It was with the recent development of sensitive psychophysiological-measurement techniques that we have witnessed impressive progress in the understanding of covert behavior. Past psychology has clearly dealt primarily with the relation of organismic behavior to stimuli of the external environment, and we can expect equally impressive understanding of our internal world, to which psychology has vigorously turned.

The classical distinction between overt and covert behavior is not a sharp one. Overt events like waving the hand or speaking aloud are apparent; but just as clearly, there are events that are hidden from ordinary observation, such as a slight thumb twitch, the brief contraction of a small muscle in the tongue, or an increase in cardiac rate. A twilight zone intervenes between these extremes. There we find events that are difficult to classify as being either overt or covert—for example, a slight whisper, a partial blink of the eyes, or an arrested nod of the head.

Whether events are clearly overt or fall within the "twilight zone," however, is in principle unimportant to us. The fact that specialized apparatus is required for the observation of small-scale behavior does not mean that covert behavior differs in kind or quality from overt behavior. Nor is it theoretically relevant that events in the "twilight zone" may be studied more effectively by the methods of covert behavior than by the classical methods of observing overt behavior. The important point is that the task of psychology is to understand behavior—*all* behavior. To accomplish this task, we must concentrate some of our energies on that subrealm of behavior that is "covert."

There is no problem, of course, in observing overt responses—difficulties arise only insofar as recording and measurement techniques are concerned. Covert events, on the other hand, can only be observed through the use of equipment that, so to speak, extends the scope of our senses. That magnification is required in order to observe phenomena is, of course, not unusual, and we have developed numerous kinds of apparatus that allow us to detect events that could not otherwise be studied. The microscope and the telescope are obvious examples and serve to emphasize that covert processes are in no sense mystical simply because they must be amplified for study. Our general focus will be on methods by which covert processes are sensed, amplified, recorded, and quantified.

The frequent reference in the psychological literature to "covert behavior" (and to similar terms like "implicit response," "subvocalization," "silent speech," and "inner speech") attests to the historical and contemporary importance of concepts of covert events. Our primary purpose here is to psychophysiologically study the various kinds of covert processes. Our long-term goal is to soundly develop the concepts and principles that will constitute a mature science of covert processes and, hence, a more complete science of psychology than one built merely on overt behavior.

3
EARLY PSYCHOPHYSIOLOGY

The various activities of the body involve chemical, mechanical, and electrical processes. Measures of chemical reactions are best left to the biochemist and physiologist. In psychophysiological research, numerous measures of mechanical reactions have been used. The mechanical measurement of covert behavior started in the early 1900s, when experimenters enthusiastically and creatively sought objective evidence of "implicit language habits," a critical concept in behavioristic theories of thinking. Techniques to record covert speech activity during thought involved such devices as inflated balloons and flattened wine glasses placed on or about the tongue; such "sensors" then had mechanical connections to recording systems of tambours and kymographs. The extreme of mechanical measurement was Thorson's (1925) device that magnified tongue movements by a factor of about 4.5 (Fig. 1). It is obvious that during the first quarter of this century, adequate technology was simply

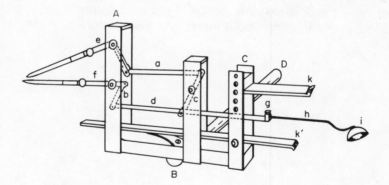

FIG. 1. Thorson's experimental apparatus (X4.5). *ABC:* rigid frame supported in adjustable clamp by the rod, *BD, i:* metal suction cup for attachment to tongue. *a:* aluminum bar, attached to suction cup by the aluminum wire, *h,* adjustable by the set screw, *g,* and transmitting movements through the links and bell cranks, *b, c, d,* and *e,* to the writing points. The writing points are adjustable horizontally by thumb screws, *m,* acting against light bronze springs. (*From Thorson, 1925.*)

lacking, and it is amazing that early experimenters ever did report successful measurements of small-scale, covert processes. The technological breakthrough came in the 1920s with Jacobson's (1927) pioneering electrical measurements of covert behavioral events and with Berger's (1929) electrical measurements of brain events. In 1908, having begun the development of his methods of progressive relaxation, Jacobson needed a sensitive measure of muscular tension as a criterion for degree of improvement of his patients. His first index of tension was a kymographic measure of the amplitude of the knee jerk response, a reflex that does not occur in the well-relaxed person. Later Jacobson employed a string galvanometer, the primitive electromyograph believed to have been first used by Forbes and Thatcher in 1921 (Jacobson, 1973). To use the string galvanometer, one inserted electrodes into muscles; the voltage generated by active muscles would produce vibration of a wire whose shadow was recorded on photographic paper.

The string galvanometer lacked sufficient sensitivity for Jacobson, who required a measure of amplitudes less than a microvolt (one-millionth of a volt). His ambitions seemed incredible to physiologists of the 1920s: The Nobel scientist, H. S. Gasser, after listening to Jacobson's extremely sensitive equipment requirements, responded by saying, "I take my hat off to a microvolt." In collaboration with Bell Telephone Laboratories, Jacobson eventually developed the integrating neurovoltmeter, which he used successfully both in his scientific and clinical work. Contrary to opinion of the time, Jacobson showed that muscle tonus could be reduced to a level of zero microvolts by the use of progressive relaxation technics (Jacobson, 1929). His use of the neurovoltmeter in scientific investigations in the 1930s allowed him to conclude that muscle responses were present during all mental acts.

In these early days, scientists were not sure what their electrical measurements indicated, as in the controversy over "Berger waves." In this regard, Jacobson (1932) established differences between covert electromyographic movement and the galvanic skin reflex (GSR). Among the differences he noted were the greater voltages of GSR readings as opposed to the much smaller voltages obtained in EMGs, the latencies of from 1.0 to 4.0 sec obtained with GSR as contrasted with the fraction of a second that commonly intervened between signal and EMG measurement of muscle activity, as well as the differences in frequency, wave form, direction of potential, and tissue of origin of GSR vs. EMGs. Jacobson's pioneering work has led to great advances in electromyography, as has Berger's well-known research in electroencephalography.

NATURE OF BIOELECTRICAL PHENOMENA

To understand the nature of electrical events in nerve, muscle, and gland cells (as well as in many plants), it is important to note that all of these cells are enveloped by membranes. In a resting cell there is a difference in electrical potential between the inside and the outside of the cell's membrane, such that the inside is electrically negative relative to the outside. Geddes and Baker (1968) have summarized a number of studies in which membrane potential differences have been measured under a variety of conditions in a variety of mammalian cells. These vary from a low of 45 mv (millivolts) in the giant axon of the squid (excised in sea water) to about 100 mv in skeletal muscle fiber of the rat *in vivo.* Eccles (1953) also discussed values of resting membrane potential differences.

When a stimulus is applied to the resting cell, an electrical event called an *action potential* is generated. The action potential occurs because the stimulus produces a localized depolarization that is propagated along the cell. Depolarization of the cell itself is due to an exchange of ions through small openings in the cell's membrane. The openings are sufficiently large to allow the passage of the cell's smaller ions from the inside of the membrane to the outside (and vice versa), but the openings are too small to allow a similar passage of the larger ions. Because its construction selectively controls the passage of ions, the cell's membrane is referred to as *semipermeable,* a characteristic that is important for an understanding of the biochemical and electrical components of action potentials. Biochemical cellular analysis is not required here (see Eccles, 1953, on this topic). We shall merely note some of the electrical phenomena that are relevant for the electrical recording of covert processes.

The propagated depolarization due to selective ionic movement may be electrically sensed in the single cell by inserting one cellular electrode inside the cell and placing a second electrode on the outside. The recorded action potential consists of several components: First, there is a small prepotential, followed by a discharge (depolarization), during which the inside of the semipermeable membrane becomes positive relative to the outside. Finally, there is a recovery (repolarization) phase during which the inside once again becomes negative relative to the outside, and the cell voltage returns to its resting membrane potential. During this recovery phase, the rate of repolarization slows, in some cells, resulting in what is called a *negative afterpotential.* In other cells, the repolarization process may "overshoot," resulting in a *positive afterpotential;* some cells even undergo a second negative afterpotential prior to returning to the membrane resting state (Geddes & Baker, 1968). In short, these are the action potentials that are sensed by electrodes placed in or on the body, and it is this electrically sensed event that produces a signal that is transmitted to amplifiers for further processing.

The actual form of the recorded action potential varies with a large number of factors; these include the particular cell, which has its special parameters for depolarization and recovery, the speed with which the propagated depolarization is transmitted along the cell membrane (fast in neural tissue, slow in muscle cells), the orientation of the electrodes with regard to the source of the action potential, and so on.

AN OVERVIEW OF COVERT PROCESSES

In Table 1, we present a number of the more commonly measured events studied in cognitive psychophysiology, noting too that a mature science of covert processes no doubt would include a variety of other measures. We start with the primary division between (I.) response events and (II.) neurophysiological processes, such that the general term "covert processes" (or equally "covert events") includes both behavioral and nervous system phenomena. After the basic division of covert processes into responses (muscular and glandular events) on the one hand, and central nervous system (CNS) reactions on the other, we observe that muscle responses are best measured through electromyography, whereas brain events are often studied through electroencephalography. This separation of response and CNS reactions indicates that the two classes of events operate differently and *are* different components of neuromuscular circuits that function during internal information processing. Although we use similar electrical methods for studying the two classes of bodily events, responses obey different laws than do neural events. It is, then, most efficient to classify systems of responses versus CNS reactions separately and to study the interactions of these events within neuromuscular circuits. Within the first major classification of responses, we shall focus on skeletal (as contrasted with smooth) muscle responses, eye responses, and respiration. A secondary division then separates responses in the oral regions of the body (I.A, in Table 1) from the nonoral bodily areas (I.B). The reference to covert *oral* responses does not commit us to any particular functional interpretation of those response events. An oral response may involve speech, in which case it is a *linguistic* oral response; or it may serve no internal information processing function (e.g., a swallow or bite of the lips), in which case it is a nonlinguistic oral response. Elsewhere we have offered an empirical justification for the conclusion that certain classes of covert oral behavior function linguistically (McGuigan, 1978).

Most of the available data on covert oral behavior have been gathered through electromyographic recording. During linguistic processing, the tongue yields the most sensitive

TABLE 1

A Summary Classification of Psychophysiologically Measured Covert
Processes (Estimates of signal characteristics are for humans)

The two major classes of covert processes are:
  I. covert responses, which consist of, and only of, muscular and glandular events; and
  II. neurophysiological processes, principally measured in the normal human through electroencephalography.

  I. Covert Responses
    A. Covert oral responses
      1. Skeletal muscle electromyographic measures (2 to 3000 Hz), principally from the following regions:
        a. tongue
        b. lip
        c. chin
        d. laryngeal
        e. jaw
      2. Pneumograms (12 to 20 respirations/min)
      3. Audio measures of subvocalization ("whispering") (20 to 20,000 Hz)
      4. Salivation
    B. Covert nonoral responses
      1. Skeletal muscle (2 to 3000 Hz) electromyographic measures:
        a. finger
        b. arm
        c. leg
        d. etc.
      2. Visceral muscle activity (electrogastogram, DC to .6 Hz; .5 μv to 80 mv)
      3. Eye responses:
        a. electrooculogram
        b. electroretinogram
        c. pupillogram
      4. Cardiovascular measures:
        a. heart rate (45 to 200 beats/min)
        b. electrocardiogram (.05 to 8 Hz; 10 μv to 5 mv)
        c. finger pulse volume (DC to 30 Hz)
        d. blood pressure (DC to 200 Hz)
      5. Electrodermal measures [galvanic skin response (1-K to 500-K resistance), skin conductance, etc.]

  II. Neurophysiological Measures
    In the normal human, electrical activity is studied and recorded with a variety of techniques [e.g., electroencephalograms (DC to 100 Hz; 10 μv to 100 μv), evoked potentials, and contingent negative variation (the "expectancy" wave)]. Other measures should also be considered, such as magnetic sensing systems (e.g., Kolta, 1973).

data; the lips appear to be the next most sensitive region; and the jaw, chin, and laryngeal regions are relatively insensitive (see e.g., McGuigan, Culver, & Kendler, 1971; McGuigan & Pinkney, 1973.) Pneumograms (I.A.2) are potentially very important measures of covert oral responses but they have not been extensively studied. Breathing rate has generally been found to increase during such linguistic tasks as silent reading, but the interpretation of this finding remains uncertain (e.g., McGuigan, Keller, & Stanton, 1964). Breathing amplitude has been found to increase during auditory hallucinations (McGuigan, 1966). Audio measures of subvocalization (I.A.3) have been extremely interesting in the study of covert oral behavior. For example, by monitoring highly amplified sounds issuing from their mouths, it is possible to understand portions of the prose that children silently read (e.g., McGuigan et al., 1964), or portions of the verbal content of a paranoid schizophrenic's auditory hallucinations (McGuigan, 1966). As an indicator of covert oral behavior, the salivation measure (I.A.4) has not been greatly exploited, but it has led to some interesting findings with regard to verbal processing (e.g., Razran, 1939).

Measures of covert nonoral responses (I.B) during linguistic processing are extremely valuable, especially EMGs from such somatic regions as the fingers, the preferred arm, and (for control measures) from the leg. Particularly interesting for us is the monitoring of covert finger activity in individuals who are proficient in dactylic language, such as deaf individuals or teachers of the deaf (e.g., Max, 1937; McGuigan, 1971). Similarly, the value of measures of covert eye behavior (especially electro-oculography, I.B.3.a) cannot be overemphasized. The last two measures of nonoral behavior listed in Table 1, cardiovascular and electrodermal recordings, are quite valuable in studies of emotion and arousal.

Various neurophysiological measures (II) should eventually lead to a better understanding of the brain during thought, but this exceedingly complex organ will undoubtedly require more advanced techniques of study than we can yet imagine.

With this overview of covert processes, we consider in the following section the psychophysiological characteristics of some of the more important covert processes in greater detail.

Research indicates that skeletal muscle responding yields the most interesting findings about cognitive functioning (McGuigan, 1978), so we shall concentrate on that covert response subclass first. We then briefly contrast skeletal muscle responding with smooth muscle activity, followed by discussions of the extremely valuable electrical measure of eye responses and of respiration. Finally, we discuss the second major category, neurophysiological processes.

SELECTED COVERT RESPONSES

6.1
Skeletal Muscle Responses

Electromyography provides the most sensitive measure of muscle activity now available, and since covert muscle responses are the most indicative of cognitive functioning, this response category requires most of our attention. The recording of muscle action potentials (MAPs) through electromyography provides the electromyogram, which is a record of the electrical properties of muscular activity.

The functional unit of skeletal muscle is the motor unit, which consists of: (1) a nerve cell body that is located in the ventral root of the gray matter of the spinal cord; (2) an axon descending down the motor nerve; (3) the terminal branches of the axon; (4) the myoneural junction; and (5) the muscle fibers that are supplied by these branches (Fig. 2).

The muscle fiber is the *structural* unit of striate muscle; in appearance it looks like a fine piece of thread. In size, muscle

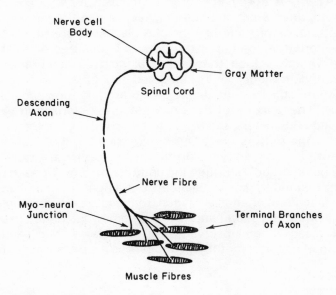

FIG. 2. Scheme of a motor unit. (*Modified from Basmajian, 1962.*)

15

fibers generally vary in length of 1 mm–10 cm, and in width from 10–100 microns, although they may exceed 34 cm in length (Lockhart & Brandt, 1937–1938). Muscle fiber components of a muscle are aligned in parallel and probably stretch from the origin as a single entity. The number of fibers per motor unit varies from several (2 or 3) for muscles whose function is fine movement (e.g., muscles in the larynx, those that control movement of the eyeball, the ossicles of the ear, etc.) to 2000 or so for muscles that perform a gross function (e.g., in the leg, the medial head of gastrocnemius).

The bodily location and the anatomical characteristics of motor units contribute to the degree of complexity of the surface EMG event. In a relatively large muscle (e.g., human biceps brachii), each motor unit is localized in an area of about 5 mm, but there are also many overlapping, intermingled, motor units within the area. Furthermore, any given motor fiber may be supplied by more than one motor neuron.

An efferent neural impulse, which arrives at the central region of a muscle fiber, produces a rapid contraction of the entire fiber (with a latency of perhaps 10 msec), providing that the impulse is above threshold (muscle fibers obey the all-or-none law).[2] A muscle fiber contraction lasts for approximately 2 msec, after which the fiber relaxes. The contraction occurs according to the general principles discussed previously (viz., the efferent neural impulse produces a localized depolarization, which is then transmitted along the membrane that surrounds the fiber; the propagated depolarization produces the contraction by stimulating the contractile substance of the fiber). The velocity of the propagated depolarization varies between 3.5 meters and 5.0 meters per sec depending on the size of the muscle fiber. During contraction, the membrane polarity is reversed, yielding the major electrical signal that may be recorded. Although the contraction time for each fiber is approximately 2 msec, all fibers of a single motor unit do not contract simultaneously. Hence, the electrical recording of a single motor unit stimulated once is somewhat longer, usually 5–10 msec. When observed on a cathode ray oscilloscope, action of a typical motor unit appears as a biphasic spike (Fig. 3).

---

[2]For a more thorough discussion of the contraction phenomenon with precise temporal values, see Gatev and Ivanov (1972).

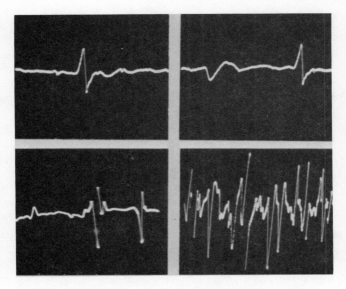

FIG. 3. A sample of normal electromyograms showing one, two, and many superimposed motor unit potentials ("interference pattern"). The single potential in the upper left corner had a measured amplitude of 0.8 mv and duration of 7 msec. (*From Basmajian, 1962, p. 14.*)

The phenomena sensed with muscular electrodes are quite varied and often extremely difficult to detect, as in the instance of very rapid or low amplitude spikes. The covert eye response detected by McGuigan and Pavek (1972) that differentiated a person's "yes" versus "no" thoughts, for instance, could not have been possible without sensitive computer analysis. Instances of these rapid response classes recently detected in our laboratory are illustrated in Figs. 4 and 5. An extremely rapid spike of .5 msec duration is shown in Fig. 6.

As the strength of muscular contraction increases, the number of motor units activated and the rate of their contraction also increases. For weak contractions, few motor units fire, and their rate of contracting is approximately 5–10 per sec. Strong contractions may produce rates of up to 50 per sec (approximately); Basmajian (1962) suggested that the rate of about 50 per sec may be the physiological upper limit for the frequency of propagating neural impulses in the efferent axon

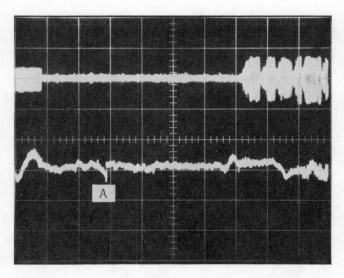

FIG. 4. The slight downward spike labeled *A* is illustrative of the eye event that occurred during silent "no" answers in the McGuigan and Pavek (1972) study.

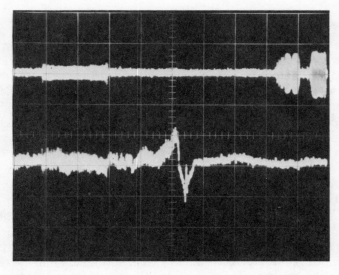

FIG. 5. The longer duration eye response in this trace is typical of a "yes-thought." *(From McGuigan & Pavek, 1972.)*

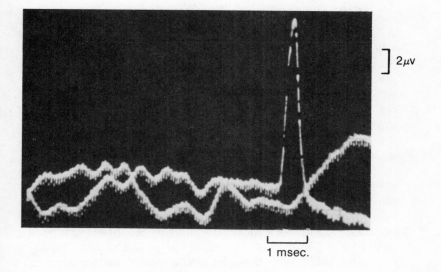

]2μv

1 msec.

FIG. 6. A monophasic spike of 10 μv amplitude and .5 msec duration, recorded with surface electrodes from the subject's leg.

of the motor unit. [However, according to Kiang (1966), spontaneous neural impulses have been measured at the rate of 100 spikes per sec, and they have been driven by external stimuli to a rate of 150 spikes per sec.]

To record the action potential given off by contracting muscle fibers, the voltage difference between two electrodes is recorded, as previously discussed. We have noted that the action potential may be detected by either surface electrodes attached on the skin or inserted electrodes (needle electrodes or hair-fine insulated wires) localized subcutaneously in the region of the muscle fiber or fibers of interest. The amplitude of the recorded signal from a given motor unit is much greater with inserted than with surface electrodes: A signal of 100 mv at the site of the origin may be attenuated to as low as 10μv when sensed by surface electrodes on the skin. This great attenuation is due to: (1) the amplitude of the signal markedly decreasing with the distance between the active fiber and the sensing electrodes; and (2) the bodily materials intervening between the muscle fiber and the surface electrodes, providing resistance to the signal. To elaborate briefly on this second factor, we may note that inserted electrodes placed just outside of the contracting fiber sense signals that are only 2–10% of the amplitude of the propagated disturbance. The signal is further attenuated as it passes through the interstitial fluid, blood, and other tissues, particularly the skin. For the placement of surface electrodes, the upper layer of the skin, which consists of nonliving cells, has a high electrical resistance; the researcher therefore should remove much of the upper layer so that the electrodes are in closer contact with the lower layer of skin, which consists of living cells that have a lower electrical resistance.

Inserted electrodes have an advantage over surface electrodes when the researcher seeks to study localized, subcutaneous events. Examples of such use come from Faaborg-Andersen and Edfeldt (1958), who studied contrasting muscle action potentials in neighboring muscles in the throat, and from Basmajian (e.g., Basmajian, Baeza, & Fabrigar, 1965), who brought single motor unit events under voluntary control [this is also possible, although more difficult, using surface electrodes (McGuigan, 1973)].

Because surface electrodes are exposed to signals from many fibers, and to a greater length of each fiber, high-amplitude electrical signals may still be detected at the surface, even though the signal from a single muscle fiber is greatly attenuated. Consequently, the surface electrode potential is a summation over both space and time. With surface electrodes being capable of detecting signals less than 1 μv in amplitude (given other suitable laboratory conditions) from a wide bodily region, they are likely to enhance the investigator's chances of detecting critical response events. Some of our standard placements of surface electrodes are illustrated in Figs. 7–12.

6.2
Visceral Muscle Activity

Visceral activity is of considerable cognitive importance, probably functioning to add "emotional tone" to semantic interpretation. Among the relatively small amount of psychophysiological research involving visceral muscle activity, there have been some interesting findings, and it is

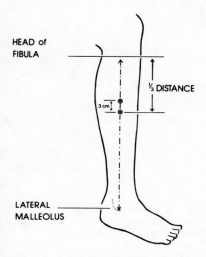

HEAD of FIBULA

⅓ DISTANCE

3 cm

LATERAL MALLEOLUS

FIG. 7. Right leg placement for EMG. (*After Davis, 1959.*)

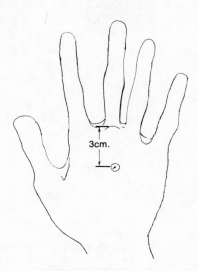

3cm.

FIG. 8. Right hand ground placement. The location on the body for grounding the subject is apparently unimportant from a recording point of view.

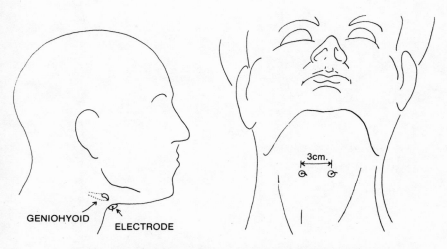

GENIOHYOID   ELECTRODE

3cm.

FIG. 9. Geniohyoid placement for EMG from the tongue with surface electrodes.

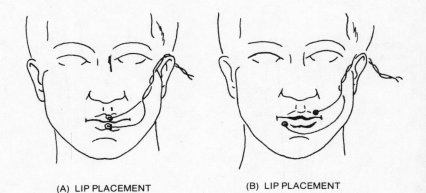

(A) LIP PLACEMENT   (B) LIP PLACEMENT

FIG. 10. (*A*) The more sensitive placement for lip EMG is directly on the lips, using stretched tape over the electrodes horizontally across to the skin. Alternatively, (*B*) electrodes may be placed above and below the lips on the skin.

FIG. 11. Vacuum electrodes may be attached to the dorsal surface of the tongue.

FIG. 12. Forearm placement for EMG. (*After Davis, 1959.*)

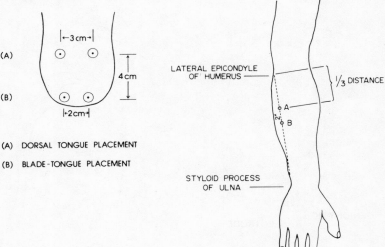

(A) DORSAL TONGUE PLACEMENT

(B) BLADE-TONGUE PLACEMENT

likely that much important linguistic-processing research will be conducted in the foreseeable future. A variety of techniques have been used for the study of these visceral events (swallowing a balloon or magnet, fluoroscopy, etc.), but electrical recording techniques are preferable because they reduce the likelihood of artifacts and appear generally more sensitive.

Electrical records of smooth muscle activity in the abdomen are referred to as *electrogastrograms* (EGG). Typically, monopolar recording is employed using either a surface or an inserted electrode affixed to the abdomen; a reference electrode is then placed at a remote location such as the forearm. For multichannel recording, several electrodes would be placed at different abdominal locations. If one does use the monopolar (as opposed to bipolar) technique, some cautions should be heeded: For example, since in monopolar recording the electrodes are widely separated (as arm to abdomen), a number of other bodily signals may be simultaneously sensed. Consequently, in monopolar recording, it is often difficult to isolate the signal of interest (here the EGG). For instance, while trying to record EGG, one may also sense respiration, bodily movements, and electrocardiograms with a monopolar arrangement, although interestingly, the galvanic skin reflex may not. Because the two electrodes are closely placed in bipolar recording, the chances of sensing artifactual signals like ECGs is greatly reduced.

As far as the frequency of the EGG is concerned, we should note that smooth muscle behaves quite differently from striate muscle. The frequency of smooth muscle activity is very low [being less than 1 cycle per second, or equally, 1 Hertz (Hz), typically from DC to about .6 Hz], and the amplitude is large [between .5 and 80 mv at the surface (Davis, Garafolo, & Gault, 1957; and Davis, Garafolo, & Kveim, 1959)].

A most interesting electrical technique for recording from the esophagus is by means of surface electrodes attached to a "swallowed" balloon, reported by Arlazoroff, Rapoport, Shanon, and Streifler (1972). The esophagus contains some skeletal as well as smooth muscle and is the primary organ for fear and chronic anxiety responses (see relaxation techniques in McGuigan, 1978).

6.3
Eye Responses

There are three fundamental methods for the objective recording of eye responses:[3]

  1. mechanical transducers in which a small rod, for example, is directly attached to the cornea.

This method is of historical interest only, having been supplanted by the following two:

  2. the optical method in which reflections of a light source onto the cornea are photographically recorded.

According to Marg (1951), this method has the disadvantages that the head is immobilized, the subject experiences a strong glare from the light source, the eyes must be kept open (blinking may spoil a part of the record), a complicated optical system is necessary if there is to be registration in two instead of one meridian, and it is time-consuming to await photographic development of the film.

  3. the electrical method of registering eye movements, which has none of these disadvantages and is the most prominently used.

Marg's (1951) history established that Jacobson (1930) was the first to use a vacuum tube amplifier for recording the changes of electrical potential during eye movement, thus launching contemporary electro-oculography. The value of the technique was confirmed by Mowrer, Ruch, and Miller (1936) with surface electrodes. Jacobson (1930, 1932, 1938a, b) measured changes in the potential of the eyes during mental activity and described the functional relationship between eye

---

[3]We exclude here discussion of casual observational techniques such as the "peep-hole" method, in which the eyes are observed through a small hole in the screen that separates the subject from the experimenter. We also exclude the recording of the illumination potential through electro-retinography (Armington, 1974) and pupillography; the former probably is relatively unimportant for the study of cognitive processes, and the latter, being an autonomic event, is not emphasized here. For a review of pupillometry research, see Goldwater (1972).

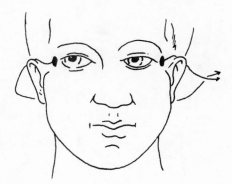

FIG. 13. Eye electrodes may be placed at the external canthi for recording primarily horizontal activity.

movements and dream content. Aserinsky and Kleitman (1953, 1955) stimulated the recent surge of research on rapid eye movements during the dream state, so that electrical measurement of covert processes during dreaming has become a major contemporary interest.

If, as is most common, electrodes are placed just posterior to the external canthi of both eyes (Fig. 13), several electrical signals may be recorded. One signal of major interest originates in a potential difference between the cornea and the retina of approximately 1 mv, the cornea being positive due to a negative potential associated with the higher metabolic rate of the retina. This is referred to as "the standing potential," first reported by duBois-Reymond (1849). The electrodes are placed directly posterior to each eye, anterior to the temples, approximately equidistant from the cornea and the central region of the retina. When the eye moves, the position of the eyeball departs from a mean zero point in the horizontal plane between the electrodes. In this case, the positive pole of this potential approaches one electrode, and the other electrode is approached by the negative pole, producing a potential difference between the two electrodes. Measurements of these variations constitute what is called the *electro-oculogram* (EOG). Hence, eye movements in the horizontal plane produce a transorbital potential that may be led into amplifiers and recorded.

Horizontal EOGs may also be recorded by placing electrodes on either side of *one* eye, rather than posterior to both eyes. Vertical *as well as horizontal EOGs,* may be obtained by locating additional electrodes above and below one eye (as in Fig. 14).

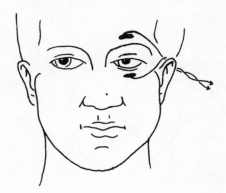

FIG. 14.   Vertical eye electrode placement.

The EOG signal is a direct current potential, hence DC amplifiers should be used for greatest fidelity. However, AC amplifiers suffice for most work, particularly if one wishes only to determine whether or not a response has occurred or merely to record frequency and direction of eye movements. DC recording is difficult because of the problem of drift inherent in the use of DC amplifiers. AC recording eliminates this problem. If one is interested in recording a linear response, DC recording is necessary since the AC method leads to sizable deviations from linearity, especially when the eye movements are greater than about 30°. A comparison of AC and DC eye-movement recordings is offered by Tursky and O'Connell (1966). Young and Sheena (1975) suggested that in *electro-oculography* one employ the DC recording method for determining eye *position.* For measuring eye *movements,* AC recording is employed—a method referred to as electrony-stagmography (ENG). The term "electro-oculography," however, is increasingly employed to refer to any electrical recording from the eyes, including the use of AC amplifiers, whether wisely or not. An illustration of a difference in AC and DC recording is presented in Fig. 15.

The researcher interested in recording only the DC electro-oculographic signal should be aware of artifacts in the form of other signals that may be sensed by the eye electrodes. For one, skin potentials (electrodermal measures such as GSR) are in the same frequency band as the EOGs. In addition, incidental light may change retinal activity, producing a multiphasic potential variously called *eye illumination potential, action potential,* or *photoelectric potential.*

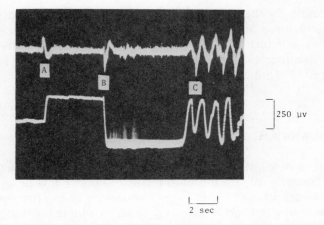

FIG. 15. Difference in traces as a function of AC recording (top) vs. DC recording (lower). The subject was first instructed to look left and hold the gaze (*A*), then look right and hold it (*B*), then "roll your eyes".

Furthermore, activity of the ocular muscles produces EMG signals, but these can be filtered out because they are of a higher frequency than EOGs. Finally, it is possible for EEGs (especially from the frontal lobes), having an amplitude of approximately 15 μv (microvolts) to be recorded as artifacts in the EOG record. However, Shackel (1967) held that there is no obvious interference from the EEG to the EOG.

Measures of covert eye responses have been extremely valuable in identifying important components of covert response patterns during a variety of thought processes. At our present level of analysis, it has been important to implicate any signal from the eye region as a component of mental activity, regardless of the technical source (EOGs, EEGs, EMGs, etc.). Electrical signals thus result not only from the EOG standing potential between the cornea and the retina, but also from numerous small saccadic movements and grosser movements that can be directly observed. Lindsay and Norman (1972) classified these complex eye movements into four categories: (1) very small and fast responses that occur 30 to 70 times each sec; (2) large oscillatory movements; (3) slow drifts of a few visual minutes one way or the other; and (4) rapid jerks with amplitudes of about 5 minutes apart, often correcting for the slow drifts. Refined analysis can isolate the precise source of composite signals from the eye, if and when desired. For further information on electro-oculography and other techniques of recording eye movements, see Kris (1960), Peters (1971), and Young and Sheena (1975).

6.4
Respiratory Responses

Sensitive respiration measures can yield valuable covert oral data because of the intimate participation of the breathing mechanism in speech activity. The source of the respiratory signal is the change in the lung capacity that is produced by contraction and relaxation of the intercostal and abdominal muscles.

A common pneumograph consists of a rubber bellows that, on expansion, increases the air pressure in a tube that leads to a device such as a pressure transducer; on contraction, the air pressure in the tube is lessened. The changes in pressure act on a sensitive rubber diaphragm, which controls one arm of a Wheatstone Bridge in the pressure transducer; the pneumatic signal is thus converted to an electrical signal that may be directly entered into an amplifier.

Another pneumographic arrangement is to place a strap around the chest, with a spring connecting the straps at the back. As the chest expands and contracts, the spring, which is attached to a strain gauge, moves accordingly. The resistance of the strain gauge is changed as the spring bends, and the resistance changes are converted by means of a Wheatstone Bridge to an electrical signal.

A different pneumographic technique is to position a thermistor below the nose to sense the temperature of the air exhaled: As the heat status of the thermistor changes, a signal from the thermistor may be transduced and recorded.

If one is interested in measuring amplitude of respiration, such mechanical and temperature systems unfortunately do not provide a linear output. Consequently, they are mainly useful for relative amplitude changes as a function of experimental conditions or for frequency measures (frequency is commonly converted to respiration rate, which for adults is generally 15–19 respirations per minute, although in a well-relaxed individual it may drop much lower).

If one does require that there be a linear relationship between respiratory amplitude and the output of the recording device, a mercury strain gauge in combination with a versatile plethysmograph can be used. Such a pneumographic arrangement is quite sensitive and can provide momentary relative amplitude changes as a function of brief experimental conditions. Sensitive pneumographic recording can yield valuable direct speech components, particularly when used in conjunction with EMG recordings from the intercostal muscles and those in the higher speech regions. Some very interesting relationships have been found between the activity of the subglottal system, the intercostal muscles, and spoken syllables. These illustrate the possible uses of the pneumogram in the study of covert processes and speech (Ladefoged, 1962).

7
NEUROPHYSIOLOGICAL PROCESSES

Our major source of information about neurophysiological activity in the normal human derives from electrical reactions recorded from the surface of the skull. The first tracings of electrical activity from over the human skull were published by Hans Berger (1929), although he had difficulty in finding acceptance for his conclusions among the scientific community. As Lindsley (1969) pointed out, neurophysiologists of the day were reluctant to think that any events other than the well-known spike potentials occurred in the nervous systems. Acceptance of the slow alpha potentials occurred only when confirmed by Adrian and Matthews (1934), no doubt also aided by the prestige that Lord Adrian added to the cause. Even then, those who did believe that the signals were generated by the brain regarded them as rather dull because the alpha frequencies were so constant and thus could not be indicative of momentary thoughts. (See, Lindsley, 1969, pp. 2–15, for some of these important historical developments in electroencephalography.) Today the controversy as to the source of alpha waves continues. We have for instance, the startling conclusion by Lippold (1970a, b, c; Lippold & Novotny, 1970) that alpha waves are generated by the eyes and resonate from the back of the skull.

Certainly there is no consensus as to the principles by which 10 billion cerebral neurons generate the various brain waves. Although we appear to be making good progress in electroencephalography, we must recognize that brain events constitute, in all probability, the most complex phenomena in nature and probably will be the last to yield to an adequate understanding. To begin to appreciate the complexity of the brain, and of its interaction with the rest of the body through neuromuscular circuits, and to gain an indication of information-processing abilities of the body, we may note, as an example, that there are 130 million rods and cones in the eye. These cells make junction with 1 million nerve fibers; this ratio of 130 to 1 indicates that exceedingly complex events must occur in the transfer of information from the receptor to the optic nerve. On the motor side, the oculomotor nerve contains 25,000 fibers, and the muscles that produce eye movements have approximately three muscle fibers for each nerve fiber. This ratio of one neural fiber to three muscle fibers invites thought about the transfer of information back from the brain to the eye musculature. For comparison with the optic and oculomotor nerves, other cranial nerves contain about 70,000 fibers, and motor roots of spinal nerves contain about 100,000 fibers. The 10 billion cerebral neurons make perhaps 5×10^{14} (i.e., 500,000,000,000,000) synapses in the cortex (C.U.M. Smith, 1970). We don't know how many muscle fibers there are, but there are approximately 1030 muscles that constitute almost half of the weight of the human body. Such sample statistics should make us quite humble in our efforts to understand the nature of the brain and particularly its complex interaction with the exceedingly complex peripheral organization of the body.

Brain waves have been classified primarily by their frequency range, possibly because the amplitude values are so much more variable among people. Approximate defining frequency ranges for various brain wave classes are presented in Table 2. Theta rhythms apparently appear earliest in humans, being recordable during the first year of life. Basic alpha rhythms emerge during the second or third year, but the faster components of alpha frequencies usually do not appear until about the seventh or eighth years of life (Kleitman, 1960). The amplitude of EEG signals is usually within 1–100 μv at the surface of the scalp, although it may reach as high as 500 μv.

Controversy continues as to the precise principles governing the generation of the various EEG frequencies, but it *is* commonly accepted that the electrical signals originate in cerebral tissue, which is an electrolyte in which chloride and

TABLE 2

Classes of Electroencephalographically Recorded
Brain Waves Defined by Their Frequency Ranges

Brain Wave Class	Frequency
Sub-Delta	0– .5 Hz
Delta	.5– 4 Hz
Theta	4– 8 Hz
Alpha	8–13 Hz
Sigma	13–15 Hz
Beta	15–30 Hz
Gamma	30–50 Hz

sodium are the main ions. The brain, not being equipotential throughout, produces potential differences that may be sensed by EEG electrodes. As with electromyograms, the main source of resistance when using surface electrodes is the skin—in this case, the skin on the scalp. Similarly, skin resistance may be reduced through abrasion, etc. The use of inserted electrodes obviously avoids the problem of skin resistance.

Potential changes tend to concentrate in one region of the brain. Alpha frequencies are greatest in the occipital lobe, so that alpha amplitudes decrease with distance from the occipital region. Electrical potentials differ as a function of brain region, so that it is common to place a number of electrodes on the scalp and simultaneously record a number of signals. Standard electrode placements are indicated in Fig. 16. For monopolor recordings, it is common to place the distant (reference) electrode at the ear lobe (A_1 in Fig. 16). For bipolar recordings, the two electrodes should be placed close to each other but with no direct (short-circuiting) contact.

Efforts to develop lawful relationships involving the ever-changing patterns of electrical gradients generated by the brain have resulted in a wide variety of methods of analysis. Classification of brain waves through complex frequency analyses and the plotting of gradients are illustrative techniques.

One popular method for studying the electrical activity of the brain is that of averaging evoked potentials from the human scalp, yielding an event that is not apparent in the spontaneous EEG. In 1947, signal averaging was developed by Dawson, who superimposed a number of synchronized EEG traces (evoked by a common stimulus) on a cathode ray oscilloscope and recorded the traces on a single photographic record. In this way, a consistent time-locked relationship appears as a consequence of the commonality of the individual traces in the group of traces, revealing the evoked potential. The importance of Dawson's work was that it led to improved methods for recording evoked potentials (viz., signal averaging with the use of small commercial computers that calculated average transients). A veritable flood of research on the evoked potential has followed. For further information about evoked potentials, see especially Donchin (1969), Goff,

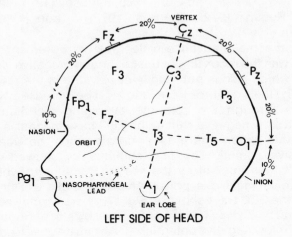

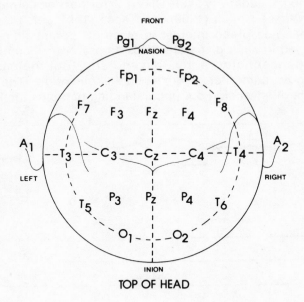

FIG. 16. International (10-20) electrode placement system for EEG.

Matsumiya, Allison, and Goff (1969), Lindsey (1971), Lindsley (1969), Regan (1972), Shagass (1972), Sutton (1969), and Vaughan (1969).

Another major advance in electrical measurement of brain activity was the recording of the contingent negative variation (CNV), which also is not readily observable in the raw trace. Typically, the signal-to-noise ratio must be increased, which is possible through the computer-averaging technique. The CNV is a slow negative shift in the EEG baseline that is readily recordable when there is a contingency between two successive stimuli. The first stimulus is followed after a constant time interval by the second stimulus to which the subject must make a response. An example of the CNV can be seen in the EEG trace shown in Fig. 17, where we may note that a light flash (S_1) was followed in 1.5 sec by a continuous tone (S_2). The slow negative potential (CNV) can be observed within the S_1–S_2 interval. The subject's key press terminated the tone and also the negativity of the CNV. For further consideration of the CNV, see Cohen (1969) and Tecce (1971, 1972).

The widespread interest in electrical potentials may be witnessed in such disparate fields as psychiatry, neurology, electroencephalography, psychology, ophthalmology, audiology, computer science, and engineering. The early promise of advancing our understanding of brain functioning

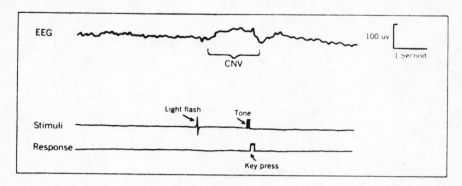

FIG. 17. Example of contingent negative variation (CNV) in the raw EEG trace. CNV is the upward shift in EEG baseline occurring between light and tone. Scalp placements are vertex (Cz) and the right mastoid. Relative negativity at Cz is upward. (*From Tecce, 1971.*)

through these electrical techniques has been realized to some extent, but we should recognize that the field is still in its infancy, as can be noted from general reviews of the literature (see, e.g., Ellingson, 1956; Karlin, 1970; Lindsley, 1944; Schmitt, 1970; and the Society Proceedings of the American Electroencephalographic Society, 1972). Ellingson (1956), for instance, concluded that too many functions have been attributed to the alpha rhythm, as in understanding the higher mental processes. Similarly, Lindsley (1969) said "I am afraid, unfortunately, that we don't know so very much more about the nature of the alpha rhythm or the other rhythms than Berger so ably described [p. 3]." Our lack of advanced understanding of electrical cerebral rhythms is also revealed through the critical review of the literature by Brumlik, Richeson, and Arbit (1966/1967), in which they categorize existing theories as being of the neuronal, mechanical, or combined variety.

This completes our survey of some of the principle covert processes that are psychophysiologically measured during cognitive functions. Since electrical components of these covert processes are most prominently sensed, the term "electrophysiology" is frequently used to denote this area of study; but because we are interested in psychological processes, perhaps for us the term "electropsychology," as employed by Hefferline, Keenan, Harford, and Birch (1960), is the more appropriate. For them, "electropsychology" refers to the study of those small-scale bodily events that occur during cognition.

It is particularly within the last several decades that extremely versatile electronic systems have been developed to allow sensitive electrical recording of signals generated by the body, and it is the electrical measurement of covert processes that has yielded the most valuable findings. As a consequence, the psychophysiological study of covert processes has been progressing exponentially.

We now turn to the laboratory system required for electropsychology. The purpose is to offer long-range guidance, and it is recognized that a full-fledged laboratory cannot be built "from scratch" without considerable practical experience. The researcher who is not yet deeply emersed in this field might find excessively demanding some aspects of the following discussion of constructing a laboratory. For them, perhaps the white rabbit's advice to help Alice find her way out of the tunnel is appropriate (viz., start at the beginning and keep going until you reach the end). For this purpose, we first consider the development of a simple and inexpensive laboratory for the study of covert processes, after which we elaborate on various points of the overall laboratory system.

8
LABORATORY TECHNIQUES FOR MEASURING COVERT PROCESSES

There are four essential features of an electropsychology laboratory for the study of covert processes: (1) sensors, which detect the signals of interest; (2) amplifiers, which modify the signals sensed; (3) readout devices, which display and record the signals; and (4) quantification systems, which render the analog signals into numerical values.

8.1
An Inexpensive Laboratory

The researcher who is just starting in this field is probably poorly financed and often must start with what is easily available.[4] Although one constructing his or her own laboratory cannot expect to start with a sophisticated one (it might even be to their disadvantage to do so), one *can* profitably start somewhere. Where one starts and how far one advances depends principally on one's ingenuity and motivation, and to a lesser extent one's research funding. The dedicated researcher will almost always find a way. For sensors, one could employ quite inexpensive electrodes (such as some offered by Grass Instrument Company), and one can also find inexpensive amplifiers. Excellent, if dated, stock vacuum tube amplifiers (such as Tektronics 122's) are available at low cost. Those who know solid-state electronics can develop effective operational amplifiers for a few dollars. Inexpensive oscilloscopes can be obtained for monitoring, although these are not absolutely essential. The major problem comes with a recording device. Inexpensive recording systems might be purchased from suppliers that deal in used equipment or obtained free from companies like

---

[4]I well remember when I first attached a pair of electrodes to a person's face (I forget where), had her sit in my office with one amplifier (X1000), and observed the signals on an oscilloscope. Roy Lachman joined me in our first attempt to "see a thought" and asked the subject a series of questions: "What is the opposite of blue?" "What is the opposite of red" ... "What is the opposite of gray?" Needless to say, this initial effort has not been recorded in the scientific archives.

Western Electric, or from "government surplus." One could even eliminate a recording system if there is access to an institutional computer. In this case, a program for integrating signals per unit time (or otherwise quantifying signals) could allow the signals to be conducted directly into the university's computer from the amplifiers. This would provide an ideal and probably inexpensive printout system. If one does record signals as on a strip chart, the time-proven quantification system of hand measurement, as discussed later, is always available.

A variety of other problems discussed later can be effectively handled by the beginning researcher, such as the problem of external (interfering) signals. Ideally, an electronically "quiet" area (e.g., a basement) could be found for locating the laboratory. The experimenter could then start off with inexpensive copper screening, checking signals on an oscilloscope to determine the relative effectiveness inside and outside the shielding. A more effective shielding is especially treated magnetic sheets of metal available from manufacturers. Some signals may not need shielding out at all, such as those sensed in brain wave recording. Or perhaps shielding may generally be eliminated, with the effective use of filters and of differential amplifiers with a high common-mode rejection ratio.

With this overview, let us now consider the components of a laboratory in greater detail.

8.2
The Laboratory Units

In Fig. 18, we can study the four major components of a relatively advanced psychophysiological laboratory. To the left, we can note that the sensors are contained in a specially shielded subject room, and that they enter the amplifiers, located in a second room. Next we note that the amplified signals are recorded on a direct recorder and also on a data tape recorder; the signals are simultaneously monitored by cathode ray oscilloscopes (CRO) and can be displayed for detailed study on a storage oscilloscope. Finally, the signals enter a quantification system that may be on-line, or may be employed at a later time, receiving data stored on magnetic

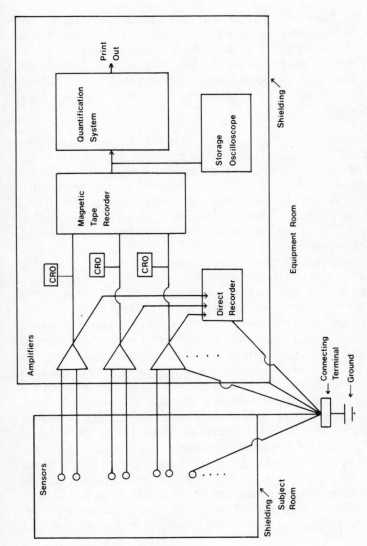

FIG. 18. A laboratory for studying covert processes, emphasizing its four major features. The shielded rooms, the shielded equipment, and the subject are all connected to a common ground, as explained in the next section.

39

tape on a tape recorder. We now enlarge on these four units in greater detail.

8.2a. Sensors. The sensor is a device that detects the signal of interest. Like a mammalian sense receptor, it is a highly specialized instrument that is especially sensitive to a given kind of energy or to a given frequency or amplitude range of a certain kind of energy. Consequently, sensors are designed so that only certain events are detected while others are rejected.[5]

Electrodes. If the event of interest has prominent electrical characteristics, then a pair of electrodes may be fixed on or in the appropriate location of the body, and a difference in electrical potential between the two electrodes may be detected. Examples of bodily events that yield electrical signals are the activities of muscles and of cerebral neurons. These two classes of events may be directly studied through electronic means, yielding electromyograms and electroencephalograms respectively.

Early electrode procedures, developed for recording electrocardiograms, required subjects to sit with their hands and feet in saline-filled buckets. An improvement made over this cumbersome "bucket" procedure was to wrap large metal electrodes in saline-soaked bandages that were applied to the skin. Eventually, electrode pastes and jellies replaced the inconvenient saline-soaked pads. However, with modern equipment for recording ECGs, concern over the nature of the electrolyte now seems irrelevant: In recording more than 4000 ECGs, Lewes used "a remarkable variety of substances as electrode jellies ... lubricating compounds (K-Y jelly, Lubrifax), culinary compounds (mayonnaise, marrons glacés, French mustard, tomato paste), and toilet preparations (hand cream and tooth paste). All of these substances are poor conductors, and all produced ECG's indistinguishable from those taken with standard electrode jelly [Geddes & Baker, 1968, p. 236]." However, while the point is a good one that

---

[5]The analogy with mammalian sense organs may be illustrated by example: The eye is particularly sensitive to frequencies in the visual spectrum; it thus rejects other (e.g., auditory) signals. Similarly, electrodes on the palm may pick up the galvanic skin response, but they are not sensitive to the pulse.

excessive concern about many laboratory procedures should be avoided, one should be careful not to over generalize from these data to other psychophysiological measures; for example, the ECG signal is of large magnitude and relatively robust compared to EMGs of less than a microvolt.

Most covert processes that are of interest here have electrical components and can be sensed directly by means of electrodes (in addition to EMG, ECG, and EEG, there is an almost endless series of abbreviations beginning with *E* for "electro," as in "electro-oculograms," "electrogastrograms," "electroretinograms"). Consequently, electrode character-istics are especially important to us. Unfortunately, knowledge about the use of electrodes in the study of covert processes is still "in the state of the art," though progress is being made. Although there are a wide variety of electrodes, only a few systematic studies evaluating them have been conducted. For a summary of several evaluative studies, see Geddes and Baker (1968, pp. 206–213). Other useful references on electrodes are Davis (1959), Geddes (1972), Offner (1967), and Venables and Martin (1967).

Surface electrodes are more widely used in the study of covert processes than are the inserted (wire or needle) type. Surface electrodes present particular problems in attempting to sense subcutaneous potentials. Cutaneous resistance is one such problem; to reduce it, a paste or jelly is placed between the electrode and the skin (Fig. 19). The paste then forms a metal-electrolyte interface between the skin and any type of surface electrode; that is, a metal-electrolyte interface is formed in which the metal is that of the electrodes, and the solution (paste) that intervenes with the body is the electrolyte. For good, accurate records, the metal-electrolyte inferface should be stable, so that there is little flow of ions from the electrode to the electrolyte, and vice versa. With an unstable metal-electrolyte interface, the flow of ions creates an artificial electrical signal that can interfere with the signal of interest. As might be expected, it is more difficult to form a stable metal-electrolyte interface with surface electrodes than with inserted electrodes. Also, movement of the body can jar electrodes, producing movement artifacts in the recorded signals that may be misinterpreted as having been generated by a bodily system. Electrode-movement artifacts can be prevented by paying particular attention to electrode characteristics, to the

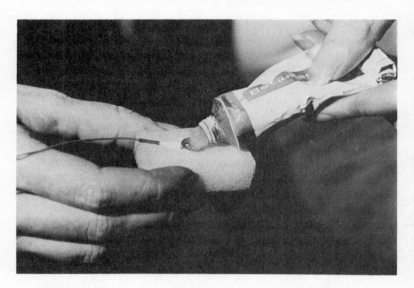

FIG. 19. Electrode jelly being applied to a surface electrode. The back of the surface electrode had been previously placed on a wet glue foam pad. The amount of jelly is excessive here for photographic purposes.

electrolyte (pastes, jellies, etc.) chosen, to the electrode attachment (placement, etc.). So that the electrode does not move about, the attaching mechanism (tape, etc.) should exert a constant pressure from the electrode to the skin surface. However, the electrode must not be attached so tightly as to cause discomfort or limit the flow of blood.

To reduce cutaneous resistance, it is especially important that the skin be properly rubbed and cleansed to remove the upper (dead) layers of skin, oil, and salt (Fig. 20). A detergent suffices for this purpose (if the skin is allowed to dry completely) and is preferable to other solvents such as ether or acetone, because the latter are flammable and constitute a danger in the presence of various laboratory sparks. When cleansing the skin, the two contact areas beneath each pair of electrodes should be kept isolated so that the cleaning and rinsing solutions on the skin surface do not make a "short circuit" between the two points; that is, residual water, soap, jelly, etc., might produce a leakage path directly on the surface between the two areas, thus attenuating the signals of interest. A completed bipolar placement is shown in Fig. 21. The foam

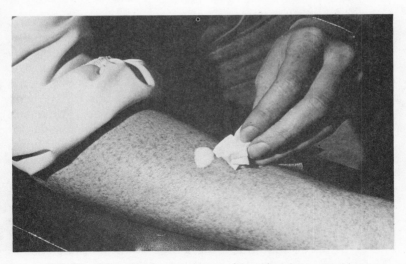

FIG. 20.   Cleansing the upper layer of the skin prior to attaching the electrode to the surface.

pad should suffice to hold the electrodes in place, but, if necessary, tape may be applied for secure attachment.

A variety of acceptable electrodes are commercially available from suppliers. Gold electrodes are quite satisfactory (inexpensive and sturdy gold electrodes are available from Grass Instruments Co.), and because of their great stability

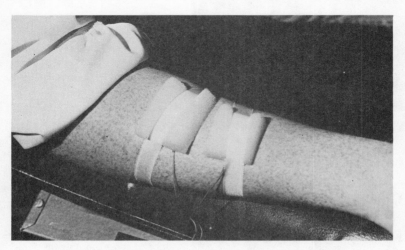

FIG. 21.   A completed bipolar attachment on the arm (see text).

(gold does not tarnish when exposed to atmospheric contaminants as silver does) are even preferable to others. Silver–silver-chloride electrodes are also electrochemically quite stable. [Procedures for putting chloride on silver disc electrodes are reported by Hill and Parr (1963).] For a specialized type of hooked-wire EMG electrode for studying activity of the intrinsic laryngeal muscles, see Hirano and Ohala (1969), and for a specialized EMG electrode for recording from the diaphragm, see Hixon, Tiebens, and Minifie (1969). For a "bathing cap" helmet for EEG electrodes, see Hanley, Adey, Zweizig, and Kado (1971).

More than one pair of electrodes should be attached to the subject so that measurements may be made simultaneously from a number of bodily locations (Fig. 22). A close-up of the tongue electrodes is shown in Figs. 23 and 24. The value of data from concomitant measures was emphasized in McGuigan (1978); one important advantage is that the procedure avoids the problem of suggestion. If only one set of electrodes is attached, the suggestion is obvious to the subject

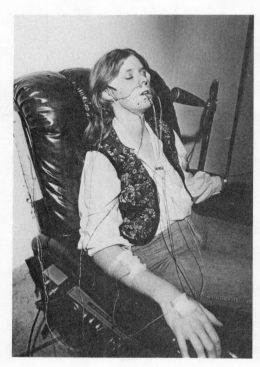

FIG. 22. A relaxing subject with several electrode placements prior to the experimental treatment.

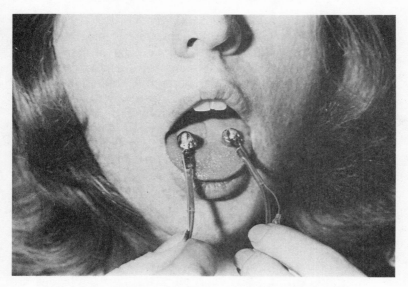

FIG. 23. A close view of a pair of suction electrodes attached to the dorsal surface of the tongue.

that something special should occur at that bodily location. Accordingly, electrodes attached only at the eyes might result in heightened frequency of blinking, and so on. If the experimenter has only one recording channel in the laboratory, then dummy (nonfunctional) electrodes should be attached at other locations of the body.

FIG. 24. The vacuum source for the tongue electrodes enters from the visible hole shown above.

Once attached, there should be a simple test of the adequacy of the preparation (condition of electrodes and paste, and how well they are applied). A straightforward observation of the signals, as on the oscilloscope, is an approximate test. To the experienced eye, the signals may or may not appear to be satisfactory; for example, alternating current from environmental circuits may impose a noticeable 60-cycle signal on the bodily signal of interest. If the preparation is inadequate, further investigation and possible adjustments are indicated, as discussed later in Section 8.8, "Troubleshooting."

Monopolar and Bipolar Electrode Placement. At our present technological level, there are two arrangements of electrodes for recording psychophysiological signals: the bipolar technique and the monopolar technique. In both techniques, the difference in potential between two electrodes is recorded. With bipolar recording, the two electrodes are placed rather close together, and the leads (wires) from each enter separately into an amplifier. If recording from two bodily regions is desired, the bipolar technique would employ two pairs of electrodes, one pair at each bodily site. With the monopolar technique, only one electrode is placed at the bodily region of interest, and a second (indifferent or reference) electrode is placed at a more remote location (such as the ear lobe, location A, in Fig. 16). Hence, in effect, only one electrode would enter the amplifier, and the potential difference between that electrode and the reference electrode would be sensed. Should recording at two bodily locations be desired with the monopolar technique, a single electrode would be placed at each location, and the potential difference between each location and the reference electrode would be recorded. When recording from several brain regions, the difference in electrical potential between electrodes over each one of those spatially different regions and the reference electrode is recorded and amplified. Consequently, the reference electrode is common for all of the channels. It can thus be seen that the bipolar placement of electrodes allows more precise recording of activity from a localized region, because the potential difference is sensed between two electrodes placed close together. In contrast, the monopolar arrangement allows the recording of relatively diffuse electrical activity that is widely spread over a larger bodily region; this is so because the distance between the electrode at the place of interest and the remote electrode is great, so that numerous signals generated by the body between the electrodes may be sensed. One advantage of a bipolar placement is that being close, the electrodes sense unwanted external signals from the environment more similarly than do the more widely separated electrodes in the monopolar arrangement (e.g., an interfering 60 Hz signal would have a similar impact on two spatially close electrodes and can be eliminated through the bipolar arrangement). Consequently, a differential amplifier is more efficient in reducing noise with the bipolar placement. Bipolar techniques are used most prominently in electromyography, whereas monopolar techniques are more common in electroencephalography. Nevertheless, depending on the researcher's purpose, either technique is appropriate.

Transducers.   A transducer is a device that changes one kind of energy into another. The story is told of a historically interesting transducer found by French engineers during a 19th-century dig in Egypt. They discovered some primitive stone and copper items within a pyramid next to the tomb of "The Wizard of Ra" and from them reconstructed the following system. An elastic animal membrane was placed over a hole at the bottom of a small tub. A sizable bulge that ran from the hole contained a mynah bird. This entire device apparently was placed inside of a large conduit that carried water from the river to the Pharoah's private bathing pools. The Wizard of Ra's device prevented the water pressure from rupturing the conduit, as follows: When the water pressure in the conduit sufficiently increased, the membrane over the hole of the tub would swell inward into the pipe that housed the mynah bird. The mynah bird then shrieked when pressed by the membrane, thereby alerting the wizard to send a runner to the river with a message to close off the water to the Pharoah's bathing pools. In this way, mechanical energy (water pressure) was "converted" (transduced) into acoustical energy, and thence into mechanical energy, terminating in water cessation.

Most frequently in psychophysiology, a transducer is used to change some physical quantity, force, or property of the body into electrical energy. If the bodily process of interest does not have prominent electrical aspects, a transducer can be used to convert its energy into an electrical signal. In measuring respiration, for example, the primary mechanical signal (a change in chest size) is commonly sensed with a bellows-type pneumograph about the chest. As one breathes, the changing chest size produces changes in the air pressure in the bellows. A rubber tube conducts the pressure changes into a pressure transducer, which emits an electrical signal that is proportional to the degree of change in chest size.

Transducing bodily events to electric signals allows us to process and display the events electronically, thereby maximizing the amount of information obtained. One can appreciate the value placed on transducing signals by noting the great number and variety of transducers that have been developed. For example, Geddes and Baker (1968) devote separate chapters to each of eight kinds of transducers: resistive, mechano-electronic, inductive, capacitive, photo-electric, piezo-electric, thermoelectric, and chemical.

8.2b Signal Modification

Amplifiers. Once an electrical signal is sensed (either directly or via a transducer), it is led from the subject to a signal modifying unit—the second aspect of the four laboratory systems. Because the signals of covert processes are of such small amplitude, the signal modification unit is an amplifier. Although the signal typically enters the amplifier by means of a small conducting cable, it may instead be transmitted by radio through telemetry (as discussed in Note #1 in the Appendix). Because amplifiers vary in an extremely large number of ways, considerable care should be exercised to select the one most appropriate for the particular covert process being studied. Amplifier requirements are primarily determined by the amplitude and frequency ranges of the signal being studied, parameters that are specified in Table 1 for certain covert processes. It is obviously essential that the amplifier have the appropriate bandwidth to process signals within the frequency range of the event of interest. For example, compared to the EMG, the ECG has an extremely slow frequency—perhaps 1 (Hz). EMG frequency, on the other hand, is in the range of 20 to perhaps several thousand Hz (considering overtones of the basic signal, too). Consequently, for EMG recording, one would select an amplifier capable of processing signals in the range between several Hz and at least 1000 Hz. As to amplitude, if the signal is relatively large (as with the ECG), then a general-purpose amplifier will suffice. For covert processes of lower amplitude (as in surface signals from the skull, or electromyographic signals of less than a microvolt), specialized amplifiers with low noise are required. It is of utmost importance that the *total* laboratory system be designed to maximize the signal-to-noise ratio. Amplifiers are critical components of that system, and, if they are of low quality, they can contribute sizably to the total system noise. An extensive discussion of the technical characteristics of amplifiers that result in high-input impedance is beyond the scope of this book; however, it *is* important to discuss the role of the amplifier in noise reduction.

Amplifiers and Noise Reduction.   Electrical noise of the amplifier may be defined as any spurious output that is not contained in the input. There are many sources of such noise. By this definition, noise may appear at discrete frequencies. For example, a 60 Hz signal may enter a system by way of an amplifier that was merely placed in the vicinity of alternating current (AC) operated equipment or power lines. Discrete signals in the radio frequency range may also arise from man-made equipment (such as a relay) operating some feet away. Shielding can prevent the sensitive electromagnetic components of the psychophysiological laboratory from being affected by stray fields from devices (motors, transformers, relays, etc.) in the vicinity. If stray magnetic fields are confined by shielding to a limited space within the device, they are being "shielded in"; if they are kept outside the device or laboratory, they are being "shielded out." Manufacturers have developed quite effective shielding systems for both purposes, and both techniques are employed in the laboratory. Well-shielded amplifiers do both: They confine internal signals (shielded in), and they sharply reduce input from external signals into the laboratory system at that point (shielded out).

Internally generated noise can also be reduced by special amplifier designs. Vacuum tube amplifiers produce two types of internal noise: white noise and microphonic noise. White noise arises from random motions of electrons and can be reduced by the use of high-quality components. Microphonic noise is internally transduced by vacuum tubes and results from any mechanical vibration to the amplifier; sound construction and a solid foundation reduces microphonic noise. Solid-state amplifiers (which use transistors in place of vacuum tubes) produce little microphonic noise, but they do produce white noise. They also produce another type of noise (referred to as "popcorn noise" or "burst noise") that is distributed randomly at frequencies less than 10 Hz. Manufacturers make available excellent amplifiers with characteristics that reduce these various sources of external and internal noise. Solid-state amplifiers are discussed further under "Operational Amplifiers" and Note #2 of the Appendix.

Amplifier specifications stated by manufacturers refer either to the input or the output stage. When specifications refer to the input, the values are independent of the amplifier's gain (gain is the ratio of output amplitude to input), whereas specifications at the output include the input effects multiplied by the gain. The experimenter should be careful to make comparisons of input specifications among amplifiers, because it is noise at the input stage that can mask the input signal. For the study of covert processes, it is satisfactory to use an amplifier that has a maximum noise level of several microvolts or less at the input stage. When noise at the output is the only specification given, divide the output noise level by the gain to find the input noise level.

With solid-state equipment, the noise level varies considerably with the impedance of the input, so noise specifications are referred to a given level of impedance. When comparing specifications of different solid-state amplifiers, be sure that the noise level is referred to an input impedance of at least 10,000 ohms; this is because we desire an electrode placement with impedance less than 10,000 ohms, as discussed later in this chapter.

There are other components of the environment than electrical signals that should also be considered, such as unwanted noises or temperature problems. In order to prevent extraneous noises from affecting the subject, the laboratory should be effectively sound deadened. A variety of inexpensive sound-absorbing materials are readily available and adaptable for this purpose. As far as temperature control is concerned, precision does not seem to be important for most purposes in the psychophysiological laboratory. Normal, comfortable temperatures seem to be satisfactory for most routine recordings, although obviously the subject should not be subjected to excessively high or low temperatures. However, if the researcher is engaged in specialized research for which temperature or humidity controls might be relevant, this environmental factor should be seriously considered. Studies of GSR require more consideration than those in which electromyography or electroencephalography is used. Certainly, too, the subject must be comfortable in terms of airflow, or any other such obvious environmental factor.

We conclude this discussion with a general point applicable to all laboratory components: It is important to have confidence in the manufacturer so that the stated specifications may be believed.

Differential Amplifiers. In addition to shielding and the use of high-quality amplifiers, there are other standard methods for reducing noise at the amplifier stage of the laboratory system. One way is to use a differential amplifier in place of the single-sided variety. With a single-sided (single-ended) amplifier, there is a single lead (wire) from the signal source (e.g., a muscle) into the amplifier. The difference in electrical potential between ground and the signal that rides on the single input lead is amplified. Because any extraneous signal in the environment may be picked up by the single lead, unwanted extraneous signals are amplified along with the signal of interest.

To understand why the differential amplifier is superior to the single-ended amplifier, let us consult Fig. 25, where two electrodes placed on the arm are represented. A differential amplifier may be thought of as consisting of two single-ended amplifiers, represented by A_1 and A_2. EMG signals (*a* and *b*) enter the two inputs. For purposes of illustration, consider signal *a*; its amplitude entering A_1 is +1 μv, a positive polarity, and entering A_2 is −1 μv, a negative polarity. Consider that the gain of A_1 is X100,000 and that the gain of A_2 is also X100,000. Hence, the output of A_1 is represented as being +100,000 μv, and the output of A_2 is −100,000 μv. In a differential amplifier, the gain is measured from the output of A_1 to the output of A_2. In this example, the difference in amplitude (100,000 times the

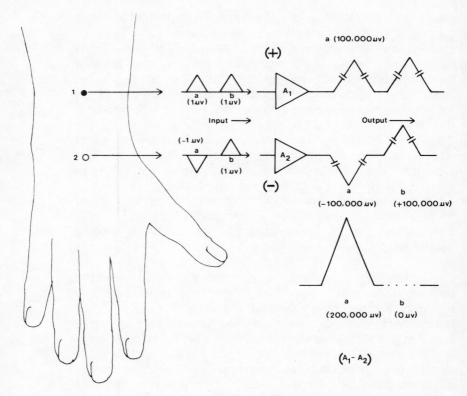

FIG. 25. A representation of the process by which differential amplifiers reduce unwanted external signals that are common to each of the two amplifier inputs (A_1 and A_2), more effectively sensing the signal. A_2 actually inverts the signal, a fact ignored here for simplicity.

input) of the two equal input voltages (one from each electrode) of opposite polarity provides an amplified signal of 200,000 μv. The result of this differential amplification is represented at the lower right of Fig. 25 as A_1–A_2, Signal a being shown as 200,000 μv.

Now consider Signal b, in which each input signal is of the same amplitude and the same polarity (the signals are thus "in phase"). The amplified signal from each single-ended amplifier is shown as +100,000 μv.

However, because there is no difference in amplitude and phase of this signal at the input stage, the output of Signal b is of zero amplitude (A_1–A_2 as shown at the bottom right of Fig.

25). Signal *b* is an example of a "common-mode signal." A common-mode noise signal in the environment that enters both inputs of a differential amplifier, being of equal amplitude and polarity, is "ignored"—as long as the noise is the same on both inputs, the output is zero. In short, the differential amplifier rejects voltages of equal amplitude and polarity (such as 60-cycle signals) that appear at both input terminals; it then amplifies the *difference* in potential between the two inputs, which ideally is the potential difference of the bodily signal of interest (the difference sensed by Electrodes 1 and 2 on the arm).

With this understanding of how a differential amplifier functions to reject a common-mode signal, we briefly consider the different degrees of ability to reject common-mode signals that a differential amplifier might have. The quantity that measures the amplifier's ability to reject signals common to both inputs is called the Common-Mode Rejection Ratio (CMRR). In the study of covert processes, an amplifier with a Common-Mode Rejection Ratio of 10,000 to 1 is sufficient to reject the usual undesired signals. (A CMRR of 10,000 to 1 means that 10 volts applied to the two inputs would result in 1 mv across the output.) In 1968, Geddes and Baker suggested that perhaps the ultimate in achieving a high rejection ratio was 300,000 to 1, obtained in a study with a number of unusual precautions. However, manufacturers now offer specifications for differential amplifiers well in excess of 300,000 to 1.

Operational Amplifiers. Another effective method of reducing noise within the amplifier is an application of negative feedback. In recent years, this application has become quite prominent in the market for amplifiers used in the study of covert processes. With negative feedback, a signal from the output of the amplifier is sent back to the input in such a way that the voltage fed back is subtracted from the input voltage, as elaborated in Note #2 of the Appendix. In contrast, positive feedback (which would be undesirable) would add to the input voltage, and, as in any system in which there is positive feedback, instability would result (as with a steam engine system in which energy is consistently added—the system would eventually go out of control).

The negative-feedback principle has been incorporated into operational amplifiers (they can be differential amplifiers), a type of amplifier that has resulted from the rapid expansion in the field of solid-state electronics. The term "operational amplifier" came from developments in the field of analog computers and denoted an amplifier circuit that performs such mathematical operations on the input as summation, differentiation, and integration. The variety of applications of the operational amplifier has by now, however, become so extensive that a listing of "op amp" functions would be large indeed. A variety of applications of *integrated circuits* for the solution of a number of basic instrumental problems in the psychology laboratory are considered by Brown, Maxfield, and Moraff (1973); see also Jackson (1975) and Tocci (1975).

Some desirable characteristics of operational amplifiers are that they produce extremely high voltage gain (primarily through the construction of a feedback loop); they have a wide bandwidth (and can thus amplify all signals relevant to the study of covert processes); they reduce internal noise (within the amplifier) and distortion; they have high input impedance (which allows current from the electrodes to be largely ignored); they have an extreme gain stability; and they have low noise at the input (less than 2 μv).

An advantage of operational amplifiers especially important for the psychophysiologist is that they can be powered by rechargeable batteries, thus freeing the experimenter from using alternating current for amplifiers. Battery operation of the amplifiers can be a big step in removing 60 Hz interference from the laboratory and can reduce shock hazards from AC leakage to subjects and experimenters as well (see Section 8.9, "Laboratory Safety"). In using battery-operated amplifiers, however, the experimenter should be careful to avoid connections between the amplifier and line-operating instruments (computers, tape recorders, oscilloscopes, etc.), because leakage currents from line-operated equipment to the amplifiers can induce ground loops and interference leakage paths in the amplifiers, resulting in 60 Hz noise (see Section 8.8, "Trouble-shooting").

One method of avoiding connections between battery-operated amplifiers and apparatus operated by AC power lines is to employ a signal isolater, as illustrated Fig. 26.[6]

---

[6]I very much appreciate George Girod's help on this point and on a number of other points throughout this section.

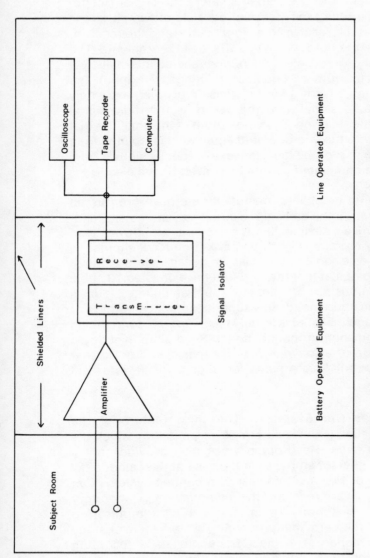

FIG. 26. A representation of how a signal isolator can be employed to prevent extraneous signals from line-operated equipment from being detected by electrodes placed on the subject.

55

The signal from the subject room enters the amplifier and goes from there into the signal isolater. The signal isolater (which can be rather inexpensive) consists of two parts: the transmitter, which receives the signal input, and the receiver, which directs the output signal to the tape recorder, etc. The transmitter and the receiver are not connected internally, yet the voltage at the output is equal to the voltage at the input. The input signal is converted by the transmitter to an extremely low-power radio signal, and the output is the radio signal detected by the receiver. Thus the output of the amplifier that is transmitted to the line-operated equipment is isolated from the foregoing part of the lab. Hence, extraneous signals from line-operated equipment cannot be sensed by the electrodes on the subject.

In developing amplifiers, manufacturers have progressed considerably from the days of the string galvanometer. Solid-state miniaturized devices like the diode and the transistor, along with integrated circuitry, have produced impressive changes in electronics. Whereas a decade or so ago a psychophysiological laboratory might have devoted 70 cubic feet to the housing of vacuum tube amplifiers, today's laboratory can house noticeably superior amplifiers within 1 or 2 cubic feet; and that area is largely taken up by the wires used for input and output connections. Solid-state electronic components are also relatively inexpensive. For further information on solid-state instrumentation, consult Note #2 of the Appendix.

8.2c. Read-Out Systems. The third feature of the laboratory system is the read-out device, a unit by which the signal is observed. Read-out devices may provide only a momentary signal for study, as in the case of the cathode ray oscilloscope, or they may consist of recording systems that provide a permanent record of the phenomenon. A laboratory typically includes both kinds, the CRO for monitoring purposes and the permanent recording system for later study of the phenomenon. The most frequently used recording system is some type of ink-writing polygraph, such as the "Electroencephalograph." (The quotation marks are used because "the electroencephalograph" is a term often loosely used for polygraphs that record a variety of psychophysiological measures besides brain waves.) Although psychophysiology has made great progress with the use of the ink-writing polygraph, this type of system is not recommended for such covert processes as EMGs, because EMGs range into the higher frequencies. The disadvantage of ink-writing polygraphs for recording such processes is that even the improved versions provide a linear (i.e., faithful) response recording only up to about 200 Hz; EMG frequencies are often too high for a mechanical recording system to follow. Another disadvantage is the inertia of the system; it does not provide a true tracing due to overlag and overshoot. For electromyograms that have a frequency range extending well above 200 Hz, a high-frequency recorder is much preferred. High-frequency recorders use an optical system, as when an input signal from the amplifier drives a miniature mirror that reflects ultraviolet light onto photosensitive paper; the signal, recorded on the paper, can then be preserved through chemical fixing processes. Such an optical system can provide a linear response recording as high as 10,000 Hz.

When direct tracings are recorded, as with ink-writing or high-frequency recorders, the experimenter's ability to quantify the data is restricted, because the phenomena can only be quantified from the paper records. For this reason, an excellent addition to a laboratory is a multichannel data tape recorder so that the signals from the amplifiers can be recorded on magnetic tape; frequency-modulated tape recorders are preferable to direct-recording tape recorders because of less distortion of amplitude and wave form and high repeatability from one playback to the next.[7] The magnetic tape may then be played into a read-out device (an ink-writing polygraph, a high-frequency recorder, or a CRO); the signals from the magnetic tape may be "frozen" for study on a storage CRO or photographed with a CRO Camera.

The data stored on tape in the original form may also be used for other methods of analysis (such as feeding them into a computer). This added flexibility is quite important because with it, the experimenter can try a variety of techniques of data

---

[7]An interesting "Pocket" portable tape-recording system is reported by Wilkinson, Herbert, and Branton (1973). The device is said to be suitable for mobile subjects; can be used to record an entire night's sleep; is suitable for EEG, EOG, and EMG; and contains its own amplifier.

analysis, some of which may be suggested only after studying the original tracings.

Incidentally, it is quite important that the recording system have several channels (or tracks) to allow the simultaneous recording of several different covert processes.

The mention of different techniques of data analysis brings us to the fourth feature of the laboratory—the quantification system.

8.2d. Quantification Systems.

Investigations conducted in the area of covert processes may be divided into two general classes: (1) those studying a brief, momentary phenomenon; and (2) those studying sustained, long-term processes. The investigator studying a momentary event is probably most interested in an amplitude measure, although other parameters, such as duration and latency, may also be important. The amplitude of the measured event should be compared to some control or baseline value to ascertain whether or not the event occurred reliably. For example, if one were trying to condition an EMG response, continuous EMG recordings would be made. The experimenter would then expect heightened EMG values following the presentation of the conditional stimulus (CS). But EMG of any bodily region is continuously (even though slightly) changing regardless of whether or not the conditional stimulus is presented. Hence, the experimenter might measure maximum height of the EMG tracing in a short interval immediately after presentation of the CS and compare that amplitude with the maximum value in a temporally equal control interval sampled some seconds prior to the CS presentation. Successful conditioning would be indicated if the CS values were significantly higher (considering a number of trials) than during the control interval (providing, of course, that adequate controls for a conditioning paradigm were employed).

In the study of longer-term records, signals may be quantified by either amplitude or frequency measures, depending on their characteristics. If the signal is cyclical and repetitive, frequency measures are typically used (although amplitude measures are not thereby precluded). For example, the pneumogram, electrocardiogram, or peripheral pulse are usually quantified by counting the number of cycles per unit time and converting to a rate, such as number of respirations, heart beats, or pulses per minute. Of course, rate is also a primary technique for classifying brain waves (Table 2).

Where the signal is not cyclical and values are required for relatively longer intervals of time, amplitude measures may be obtained in several different ways. Perhaps the simplest technique is to measure the height of the tracing with a ruler; one would thus compute peak-to-peak amplitude by measuring from the highest point of an event (like an EMG spike) to the lowest (for instance, the peak-to-peak amplitude of the event in Fig. 3 on p. 17 would be about 1.2 cm, a value that when converted to voltage is .8 mv or 800 μv).

In measuring signals over long intervals of time, data may be sampled by pre-selecting temporal intervals during which the measure will be taken. More typically, the total tracing may be subdivided into smaller time intervals; in this case, the maximum amplitude of a spike that occurs during each smaller interval (e.g., each 10-sec period of a 30-min record) is measured, and the mean of these maximum amplitude values is computed. The EMG is a good example of a record for which this procedure is used, so that changes in maximum amplitude are studied as a function of time and experimental condition.

Amplitude measures are also often taken in the case of long-term cyclical signals. For example, changes in the amplitude of the pneumogram or in the pulse record can be studied by measuring the height of each cycle with a ruler.

Hand-measuring techniques are quite simple, though typically time-consuming, and thus are often replaced by various automated procedures. An integration device (which sums the amplitude of the signal from the subject as a function of time) is perhaps the most popular procedure for quantifying sustained records by amplitude measures (integrators are typically included in standard ink-writing polygraphs). Again, the EMG is a good example of a measure for which the use of an amplitude integrator is helpful.

Integrators have been constructed on the basis of several different principles, but they all sum the electrical potentials in either of two ways: (1) they discharge a signal that is indicative of the summed potential per unit time; or (2) they discharge when their capacity has been reached, so that a standard amplitude is printed out at varying points in time. In the former case, the electrical potential from the amplifier is stored, and its discharge is triggered by a timing device at constant time intervals. Here, the electrical discharge can activate a writing pen, and the height of the pen mark is a measure of the amount of the stored electrical potential. In the second case, the electrical potential is stored until the maximum storage capacity of the integrator is reached (by the same principle as the capacitor), at which time the signal is automatically discharged and an ink pen is activated. The response-amplitude measure is then indicated by the amount of time required for the integrator to discharge its stored potential. For some integrators, the writing device provides a continuously increasing record of the amount of the potential being stored up to the point where the capacitors discharge, and the pen is then reset to zero.

In addition to recording or integrating data on line (directly from the subject without storage) by means of either low- or high-frequency recorders, we mentioned the advisability of including a multichannel magnetic tape recorder in the laboratory. The tape recorder and the direct recorder could be in parallel in the system so that the signals from the amplifier would be directly recorded and also stored on magnetic tape for other kinds of analysis. Because the stored signals are in analog form, the magnetic tape would be entered into some type of analog-to-digital conversion system so that the data may be printed out in quantified digital form. For instance, the continuous analog psychophysiological signal stored on the magnetic tape may be digitized automatically by an analog-to-digital converter such that the quantity of integrated voltage per unit time may be typed out in microvolt units. The particular analysis depends on the nature of the experimenter's problem, but a wide variety of analog-to-digital quantification systems are available. Computers that contain analog-to-digital converters are appropriate for this purpose, or more limited systems may be put together from standard units sold by electronic manufacturers. With the use of such systems, the experimenter can arrange for printing or plotting an integrated value per unit time, the frequency of the signal, an average of the signals, etc. Such analysis can also be programmed for on-line computation, providing of course that the experimenter knows sufficiently well in advance how the data are to be analyzed.

8.3
Signal-to-Noise Ratio

Several times we have mentioned techniques for reducing electrical noise in the system. In this section, we consider noise reduction throughout the laboratory system by emphasizing the general principle of maximizing the laboratory's total signal-to-noise ratio. This ratio indicates the degree to which the signal dominates the noise. Everything else being equal, the goal is to develop the largest signal possible and the smallest amount of noise.

The raw signals that the experimenter attempts to record may range below a microvolt. Such signals are extremely weak compared to those that are produced by various man-made devices likely to be present in the laboratory's surroundings. Such unwanted signals can easily obscure the bodily signal of interest. Figure 27 is an illustration of how a signal (top trace) can be covered up by noise (bottom trace); through specialized techniques, it is possible to recover the signal from the noise, but it is much more desirable to prevent noise from entering and developing within the recording system.

To maximize the signal-to-noise ratio, there are a number of feasible steps that can either increase the amplitude of the desired signal or reduce the amplitude of noise. Most obviously, the signal-to-noise ratio can be increased by increasing the factor by which the signal of interest is

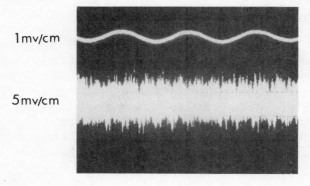

1mv/cm

5mv/cm

FIG. 27. Illustration of a signal deeply buried in noise. With special electronic instruments, it was possible to recover the upper signal from the noise buried in the lower one. (*Concept courtesy of Quan-Tech Laboratories, Inc.*)

amplified. In principle, the signal may be amplified without limit merely by adding additional amplifiers in series into the circuit. However, there are practical limits to the amount of amplification that can be tolerated. These limits are set by the characteristics of the amplifier and recording systems because, when the signal of interest is further amplified, the noise in the system also is necessarily amplified. Consequently, mere amplification is seldom productive beyond a certain factor, at which point efforts should be concentrated on noise reduction. Typical amplification factors for such covert responses as EMG range in the neighborhood of 10,000 and 100,000. Active regions, like the tongue, dictate lower amplification, whereas "control" (inactive) regions like the leg allow high amplification to be used.

8.3a. Noise Reduction.   There are two major sources of noise that are electromagnetically picked up and transmitted within the recording system: (1) signals that are generated within the laboratory itself; and (2) external signals. The former may be subdivided into those that are generated from within and from without the amplifier. As already noted, noise within the amplifier may be reduced by quality design and by the use of negative feedback. Noise generated by laboratory components outside the amplifiers may be reduced by shielding-in all equipment (this is typically already accomplished by the manufacturer); for example, amplifiers are encased in metal, and leads (cables, wires) are shielded within flexible metal conduit. The experimenter then connects the shielding of all equipment together and grounds the equipment so that the major portion of the unwanted signals generated in the equipment led into the ground (as illustrated in Fig. 18).

To reduce noise generated from outside the amplifiers, the introduction into the laboratory of equipment that functions on alternating current should be avoided if possible. DC lighting can be used throughout the laboratory (Johnson & Murphree, 1972), and as much of the apparatus that can run on DC as possible should be selected.[8] Because of the

---

[8]Although psychophysiologists are indebted to Steinmetz for so many things, his advocacy of the general use of AC instead of DC is not one of them. How much simpler the psychophysiologists' problems would be if he and his other early colleagues had selected DC for everyday use. One of the early points in favor of AC, incidentally, was that AC was preferable for electrocuting people.

omnipresence of 60-cycle current, special notch filters can be used to filter out signals in the frequency range between, say, 58 to 62 Hz. Notch filtering, of course, eliminates part of the signal of primary interest, but it is probably more important to reduce stray 60-cycle signals.

In addition to the use of notch filters for 60 Hz signals, high and low filter settings are also common on amplifiers. Many electromyographers set their low-pass filter in the vicinity of .8 Hz (thus avoiding the nasty problem of sensing DC currents that ride on the surface of the skin), and the upper filter at 1000 Hz (thus filtering out noise above that frequency). An illustration of 60 Hz interference is presented in Fig. 28. The tracings were filtered with high-pass filter settings at 10,000 Hz (top; right arm), 1000 Hz (center; left arm), and 100 Hz (bottom; left leg). All electrodes were purposely applied so that one of each pair was properly attached and the second was poorly prepared. The result was an impedance mismatch, which especially invites 60 Hz interference.

Noise from 60 Hz power lines can also be minimized (particularly in a high noise environment), by twisting together the two leads from each electrode pair along their length with about two or three twists per inch. The twisting assures that both leads receive similar signals from external sources so that the noise may be reduced through differential amplification. External noise remaining after these steps are taken may be

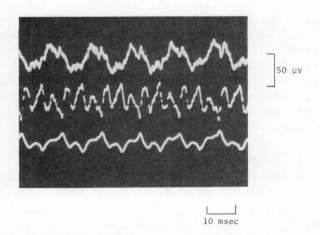

50 μv

10 msec

FIG. 28. Illustration of several forms of 60 Hz interference (see text).

further reduced by the use of differential amplifiers (as discussed earlier in this chapter).

External signals from sources outside of the laboratory may be of especially large amplitude and therefore of particular concern.[9] If the shielded room that contains the subject were 100% effective, and if the subject room contained no electrical equipment that could generate extraneous signals, then the sensors attached to the subject would detect and transmit only the bodily signal of interest, with no noise transmitted into the amplifiers. The ideal of 100% effectiveness can only be approximated, unfortunately. The closest approximation would probably be brought about by constructing the psychophysiological laboratory in a cave, far removed from man-made electrical devices. Because a laboratory in a cave is unreasonable, experimenters employ metal shielding about the laboratory rooms, as previously illustrated in Fig. 26. The most popular shield is a copper screen placed in or on the walls, but more effective (and more expensive) shielding can be obtained by using sheets of specially constructed steel (one of low and one of high permeability). The effort is to reduce unwanted 60 Hz signals as well as higher-frequency signals (e.g., radio) as much as is feasible; it might be added that the higher frequencies are the relatively easier to reduce, although they interfere less with the low-frequency psychophysiological signals with which we deal.

Special attention should be paid to shielding the subject, because any noise picked up at the initial electrode stage is amplified. Unlike the signal from the subject, noise that enters the system after the amplifiers is not amplified. Nevertheless, even though it is more important to prevent noise from entering the system prior to the amplifiers, noise picked up by the amplifiers, recorders, etc., should be minimized by shielding, which should include separate shielding about the apparatus room.

8.3b. Signal Averaging. Another technique for improving the signal-to-noise ratio is to use signal averagers, now commonly available as separate units or as adjuncts to small

---

[9]The importance of shielded rooms was forcefully impressed on me in the early days of my laboratory when I picked up Frank Sinatra through electrodes placed on the chin of my subject.

digital computers. Signal averaging is appropriate when there is a repetitive signal, but not when the signal is a unique event. Signal-averaging computers average events that are time-locked to a repeated stimulus presentation. After a number of trials, bodily signals that are time-locked to the stimulus are represented as an average output from the computer. Various random fluctuations in each individual signal add and subtract their amplitude values equally (in the long run) at any given time following stimulus presentation; hence, random fluctuations in the bodily (and other) signals over trials average zero amplitude (tend to "cancel each other out"), whereas those events that are regularly locked to the stimulus presentation add or subtract amplitude values consistently. The final summed potential is, thus, the average of events that are lawfully related to the stimulus. In short, signal averagers present stimulus-related activity that occurs repeatedly over trials and eliminates signals that are out of phase and random with respect to stimulus presentation. For instance, if a light flash is presented on a number of trials, the light stimuli may trigger the signal-averaging computer to analyze the psychophysiological signals immediately following. Brain waves are commonly averaged following a repetitive series of light flash presentations, and the averaged brain reaction may be quite precisely plotted out (even though the reaction on any of the individual trials is obscured by noise, as in the bottom trace of Fig. 27). What is common in the individual sweeps constitutes the average, whereas stray events, tending to be random, are "averaged out." The averager thus produces a single trace that is the average of the inputs of a large number of sweeps. It should now be obvious why signal averaging is not appropriate if there is but one stimulus presentation.

The technique of signal averaging is one of the major apparatus advances made in the area of psychophysiology and has produced a large number of valuable findings. Detailed methods of signal averaging, computer programs, etc., are available from the instrument manufacturers. Although signal averaging is quite effective in noise reduction, it is still preferable to reduce noise prior to the input of the averager, because the less the noise, the fewer the trials required for a good average trace.

One serious problem with signal averaging, as it is normally accomplished, has been brought to light by Dawson and Doddington (unpublished manuscript). With the use of the filtering process that is normally used in psychophysiological laboratories (referred to as "analog-frequency filtering"), the shape of the signal and its time characteristics are somewhat distorted. On the basis of some highly interesting test data, Dawson and Doddington recommended the use of interference filtering for signal averaging, a technique in which the signal is averaged upon itself. The serious researcher should consult the original work of Dawson and Doddington on this point.

8.3c. Grounding.   The grounding system is so important that if it is defective, all other techniques of noise reduction are relatively trivial. The reason is that if extraneous signals picked up by the shielding and subject are not led off into the earth, or if there is a ground loop in the laboratory grounding system, the extremely small signals generated within the body will be "masked" (obscured) and have little or no chance of being sensed.

The primary principle of grounding is that all conducting items in the laboratory should be connected together with a good intralaboratory wiring system; there should then be a single lead from that interconnected system that goes directly into the earth. In this way, electromagnetic transmissions that are picked up by the shielding of the equipment, as well as those that are picked up by the skin of the subject, can be prevented from entering the sensing and recording system by being discharged into the ground.

It is important to emphasize that the grounding wires should be attached to the shielding of each piece of equipment at *one and only one point,* so that the apparatus, the shielding, and the subject have a single common connection, which should then enter the ground *at a single point.* For instance, the experimenter would not run a ground wire from the front and another from the back end of the same equipment. It does not help to run multiple grounds from a single item of equipment. In fact, rather than helping, multiple grounds can produce ground loops that may impose a large 60-cycle signal on the psychophysiological signal. In interconnecting the equipment, it is best not to run grounding wires from one item of equipment directly to another; rather, it is preferable for the ground wire from each piece of equipment to go to a common terminal, a terminal that connects with *one* cable to the earth.

Similarly, the subject and the shielding of the rooms have but one ground wire that connects to the common terminal. This principle is illustrated in Fig. 18, with the exception that we have not indicated separate ground wires to the common terminal for each item of equipment. It is important too that all connections be well made, because loose connections may pick up interference or easily become disconnected and thus disable the laboratory system.

The cable that runs from the connection terminal into the ground should provide minimum resistance so that the external signals picked up by the shielding can be effectively conducted into the earth. An excellent ground cable would be a copper cable, ½ inch in diameter, that runs a distance from the laboratory of about 100 feet. The cable would then be connected to a metal pole that is buried about 10 feet into the earth. This may sound like an excessive precaution, but simpler grounding systems are likely to be inadequate. As an example, there are sizable differences in potential between different locations in the earth, so if the experimenter merely leads a small wire (inadequate sized) from the shielding to a metal pole driven into the earth's surface (not deep enough), he may not adequately disburse the extraneous signals picked up by the shielding; furthermore, the pole may be dislocated by a lawnmower, children's habits of kicking things, or other mysterious forces. Similarly, attaching the shielding to the water pipes of the building does not produce a true ground because a variety of external signals generated in different parts of the building may be riding on the water pipes, and these might be conducted directly back into the laboratory.

8.4
Generalizing from Psychophysiological Data

We have noted that the characteristics of any psychophysiological signal vary with a large number of conditions. For instance, there is constantly changing ambient noise in the environment, and even the most effectively shielded laboratories do not completely exclude all unwanted signals. Another important variable affecting psychophysiological data concerns electrode placement. It is unfortunate that, for both surface and inserted electrodes, precisely constant electrode placements cannot be obtained on successive sessions with the same subject, or among different subjects. For instance, if the experimenter seeks to record chin electromyograms or electroencephalograms from region O_2 (see Fig. 16), there will be some variation in the placement of the electrodes on repeated measurements of the same subject, or among different subjects. For one thing, the skin resistance will vary somewhat with the particular electrode preparation (how hard the skin is rubbed, etc.) and, for another, the resistance between the electrode and the underlying source of the signal changes somewhat even within an experimental session for a given subject. The precision with which we measure the amplitudes of an alpha wave recorded over site O_2 on the scalp, for instance, is somewhat limited—one cannot guarantee that absolute amplitudes of signals can be confidently measured to the "nth degree" among different subjects, or for a given subject at different times. Approximations to absolute amplitude values *are* possible when extreme care and experimental techniques have been exercised, but our major sources of inference in psychophysiology rest on *relative,* rather than absolute, amplitudes.

In establishing a relative amplitude, an experimenter typically measures a signal under a standard recording condition, such as a baseline value when the subject is at rest. One then compares the amplitude (frequency, etc.) of the signal under some experimental condition with its amplitude under the standard condition. Relative amplitude is thus determined by the change in a subject's behavior during an experimental session from one condition (e.g., rest) to another (e.g., an experimental condition). Typically, a representative value during the resting baseline condition is subtracted from a representative value during the experimental condition, in order to assess the effect of the experimental treatment. Sometimes a ratio (or percentage) increase over baseline is measured, instead of a difference. Because of these considerations, most psychophysiological statements about covert processes rest primarily on relative as opposed to absolute values as a function of experimental conditions. For example, one is somewhat limited in making a precise general statement that, during silent reading, right forearm EMG increases from a mean resting value of X μv to a mean silent reading value of Y μv. A sounder statement in this instance is that the mean increase in right forearm EMG was $Y - X = Z \mu v$. These limitations not only apply within each laboratory, but, due to different techniques and equipment among laboratories, the limitations are even greater when comparing values observed in one laboratory with those observed in another.

Whereas the consequence of these limitations in measurements for a science of covert processes is that our statements have some limits as to their generality, this limitation is no less severe in the study of overt behavior, where changes from baselines rather than absolute values are also the accepted standard. Great progress is still possible by studying relative amplitude changes and approximations to absolute amplitude values.

To correct for individual differences in a subject's range of response values, Lykken, Rose, Luther, and Maley (1966) developed the following ratio, which experimenters may use profitably (McGuigan, 1970).

$$\text{Ratio} = \frac{\bar{X} - \text{minimum}}{\text{Maximum} - \text{minimum}}$$

For this equation, the mean response measure $(\bar{X})$ is computed for an experimental treatment period for a subject; the minimum response amplitude of which the subject is capable is similarly computed. The latter value may be determined by a search of the entire record for a subject's experimental period. Similarly, the subject's maximum response value may be determined, perhaps by searching similarly throughout the entire record or instructing the subject to make a maximum response. The result is a ratio that can vary between 0.0 and 1.0, such that the higher the value of the ratio, the greater the subject's response amplitude. Lykken et al. (1966) have shown that this ratio corrects for individual differences in a subject's range of response values and thus may yield a more meaningful dependent variable value than what is often used.

Incidentally, in searching for a maximum response value, there might occur irrelevant artifactual responses that need to be ignored or removed from the data analysis. The subject may suddenly jerk, causing an irrelevant hand response, or may swallow or bite the lips. Such behaviors should thus be removed from the records. A variety of techniques can be developed for this purpose, but they all involve some kind of continuous monitoring of the subject during the experiment. When such irrelevant responses occur, they need to be so marked on the records and removed from further consideration. In simple on-line recording, one merely watches the subject and identifies the irrelevant response on the recording accordingly. If there is no experimenter with the subject in the subject room, then perhaps a television camera can be mounted to monitor the subject with the receiver in the experimenter room. If a magnetic tape recorder is being used, perhaps a special signal can be entered on one of the channels (either directly from the subject room or indirectly from the experimenter–apparatus room). (Should a TV monitor be used, it should be pointed out to the subject, and his or her permission for its employment should be obtained.)

8.5
Establishing a Baseline

The considerations in the previous section emphasize the importance of establishing a valid baseline. In fact, in order to ascertain whether or not some experimental treatment produces a response change, it is critical that a low, stable, resting baseline be established for the subject. If the subject is highly aroused prior to engaging in some active thought process, for instance, the experimenter would have difficulty in ascertaining whether a given covert reaction occurred during those thought processes. In Fig. 29, we note an excessively high baseline in the lips prior to the start of the experimental treatment. That high baseline may be compared with more adequate baselines in the tongue and leg. In Fig. 30, the baseline for the lips was more satisfactorily established than in Fig. 29. It is good practice, therefore, to produce a state of tranquility in the subject in order to most effectively measure response changes as a function of experimental conditions. A number of procedures can contribute to the establishment of a low-level stable baseline. For one, the concept of a psychophysiological laboratory itself may produce unwanted arousal effects, as in fear. The experimenter should therefore take all possible steps to

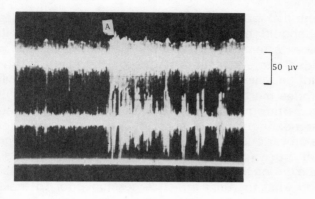

50 µv

5 sec

FIG. 29. Covert lip and tongue EMG during perception of time compressed speech (which started at *A*). From top to bottom, the tracings are from the lips, tongue, and leg. The excessively high baseline for the lips (but not for the tongue or leg) may be compared with a more satisfactory baseline in Fig. 30.

reassure the subject and to prevent any emotion-arousing terms to be used during the instructions. For instance, it is wise to make sure that the subject does not view any complex (threatening) apparatus, which can be accomplished by having the subject directly enter a subject room rather than go

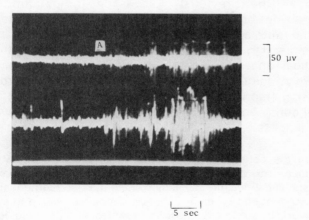

50 µv

5 sec

FIG. 30. Increased lip and tongue EMG during speech perception, as in Fig. 29. The baseline for the lips is low and stable.

through the apparatus section of the laboratory. The subject room should be appropriately decorated so that it, too, produces a restful nonthreatening effect. In instructing the individual, no suggestion that he or she might be shocked should be given, which can be avoided by referring to electrodes merely as these little "wires," or "things." Thus, when obtaining permission to attach electrodes, the researcher might say merely that "We are now going to place these on various portions of your body such as here on your arm. In no way will you be harmed." A friendly and jovial attitude during the pre-experimental phase is helpful. It is also a good idea to run a practice session prior to the actual experiment, showing the subject exactly what is going to happen in the experiment, thereby removing any anticipatory fears. Once the subject knows that "that's all there is to it," his or her habituation to the laboratory can be facilitated. Such a training session also is instructional in that it assures that the subject understand the procedures.

8.6
Some Comments on Statistical Analyses
by Mary E. Reuder and by Jeffrey A. Kadlac

Some of the previously discussed topics concerning generalizing, baselines, and assorted statistical matters can become quite complex, especially considering the infancy of our field and the difficulties of employing efficient methods of statistical analyses where our measured phenomena are relatively unique. Some incisive comments by Professor Reuder (personal communication, January 27, 1978), based on her considerable experience, are reproduced here with our special appreciation.

> In the course of doing research in the area of EMG measures during "mental work", I encountered some statistical-design problems which I later learned are encountered by many others and are not unique to my work. In fact, I found these same problems in other studies using non-physiological variables. The pertinent psychological elements which appear to be most relevant are the presence of some kind of "arousal" or "threat" (as

perceived by *S*) condition and/or certain personality factors related thereto.

The core nature of these problems is that, despite the most rigorous care in research design and data collection, the experimental procedures themselves produce characteristics within the obtained data about which mathematical statisticians have provided repeated warnings. If one violates the basic (mathematical) assumptions of a statistical technique, the mathematical approach is to state that the technique is inappropriate and "cannot" or "should not" be applied. Yet, one is in a dilemma when one has executed a very carefully planned study within the constraints of the statistical design and then finds that one or more of the empirical effects is that the experimental procedures produced the very violations one was trying to avoid. In essence, these "violations" constitute a genuine, critical research finding, despite the mathematical theory. They also pose problems as to what "to do" about them and how to interpret them.

I would like to "spell out" three of these problems that I have encountered most frequently and, on which, statistics books often give contradictory, erroneous, impractical or confusing advice. Recently I have learned that R. J. Harris in his book, *A Primer of Multivariate Statistics,* Academic Press, N.Y., 1975, has dealt with many of the same aspects of some of these problems, but at a much more sophisticated (and mathematical) level.

1. One of my most frequently encountered problems, I have also learned is a ready topic for post-mortem discussion at professional meetings. Whether using physiological or psychological dependent variables, I have come to encounter "heterogeneity of error" variance *whenever* the above-mentioned psychological "arousal" conditions are combined with a wide variety of tasks. Arousal appears to make some persons "freeze" and others to "expand" or "scatter" in their response to such stimulation. Thus, the standard deviations (and error variances) for the contingencies containing the arousal element are usually significantly greater than those which are neutral or non-arousing. This is a genuine, empirical, consistent, experimental finding and not necessarily a consequence of any violation of the basic conditions for a parametric statistical analysis, as in an analysis of variance. Statistically and mathematically, however, it means that the cell error variances and the cell means are

correlated in some way (and not necessarily linearly). Despite one prevailing statistical view that the F-test is "fairly robust" and not too seriously affected by such heterogeneity, I have found this not to be the case with the types of variables noted. Furthermore, the heterogeneity can mask significant treatment differences between means or exaggerate such differences artificially. Although mathematical transformations of the raw scores usually require much trial and error and are very tedious to resolve, I have found their use to be far more effective in evaluating experimental findings than the frequently-recommended non-parametric tests. Furthermore, transformations occasionally point up the fact that an arbitrarily chosen metric just wasn't additive, even though we thought it was. Obviously, if a suitable transformation cannot be found (and it happens), one does have to fall back on the non-parametric tests as a last resort—even though they are generally less sensitive to experimental manipulations.

2. Another problem is highly related to the first because it can be a contributing source to error heterogeneity. It also systematically runs through the literature on electromyography (as well as for other psychophysiological indices) as it relates to other facets of behavior. This is the choice of metric or unit of measurement selected for the psychophysiological variable(s) employed as the dependent measures. From the earliest reports by Max (1935, 1937), R. C. Davis (1937) and others, it was apparent that large personal individual differences in activity-level readily masked the physiological changes which might be produced by experimental manipulations when groups were compared. The very obvious "control" has thus been one of obtaining a pre-treatment sample of the EMG which can be thus used as a baseline. The problem arises from a concern as to how best handle comparisons of experimental findings with this "control" measurement. A variety of methods have been used to "correct" or "equate" for such differences in initial and/or resting level in EMG as well as other indices. When one is focused upon *individual* prediction, the very simple procedure of using an ordinary difference score between initial and final level is often the most reliable. However, this procedure does not help to equate or reduce the error term in a parametric statistical analysis. It also raises (among others) the potential problem of interpreting

possible negative changes which may make no sense in terms of the variables used in establishing the experimental design. Some persons have thus preferred to use a ratio of treatment level over resting level. There are many pros and cons to the merits of this and other ratios and metrics. The choice often appears to be based on the pragmatics of the experimental situation. It does not, in any way, take account of the situation described under 3 (below), should such relationships exist within the data. However, there is another possibility. If, as is usually the case, the relationship between the initial level and treatment level of EMG (or other psychophysiological indicator) is basically linear, a co-variance analysis in which initial level is partialled out has proven to be especially valuable. Because this technique reduces extreme values proportionately more than middle ones (assuming a reasonably high correlation), it is probably the most efficient, reliable and conservative to use when attempting to define the existence of a general type of group phenomenon. The computational techniques for handling this are clearly spelled out for the 2 by 2 design in Winer (1971). For designs having more than two levels of all variables, the procedures have been in most major books on experimental design for years [Edwards (1950), Lindquist (1953), Snedecor (1946), etc].

3. However, a word of caution is in order. Related to the above recommendation, I have frequently encountered an incipient hazard when using 2 by 2 designs. This has occurred with enough frequency (even though not a commonplace event) to warrant some serious attention. All co-variance computational formulations make an assumption known as "homogeneity of correlation." In essence, this means that the initial EMG (or other psychophysiological index) correlates with the treatment EMG to about the same degree—both from one contingency combination to the next and in the total distributions of the data as a whole. Yet, when I related personality and/or motivational variables (especially of the arousal-type) to EMG (and sometimes other dependent variables), the correlations of the initial resting level with the treatment level were not even remotely uniform. Instead, they were often heterogeneous at a p-value beyond .001. These correlations differed drastically from cell to cell. Frequently, upon examination, one could readily infer a common-sense, post hoc basis for these patterns.

There has long been available a procedural computational correction for this situation for experimental designs in which each main effect and interaction has more than one degree of freedom. However, these procedures, readily available in most textbooks on experimental design, require the loss of one *df* for each main-effect, interaction and error-term in computing the Mean Square in an analysis of variance. It is obvious that if such a procedure were applied in a 2 by 2 design, there would be zero degrees of freedom for these elements and one would artificially reduce the obtained computational values of the mean squares and *F*'s to zero.

Many years ago, Ardie Lubin and I worked out a means of handling this problem which was based upon the definitional formula for covariance. Subsequently I have been told that this is now in the general literature, but I have not come across it. Basically, it requires one to compute each Pearson Product Moment *r* (even on very small samples) for each of the cells of the four combinations of the two independent variables. Then, using this value of *r* and the appropriate regression equation, take the obtained resting-level EMG for each subject and compute a predicted value of EMG (presumably the degree of variance in the obtained treatment EMG one would expect solely as a result of the subject's own particular basic activity level). Using the appropriate *r* for each cell, the predicted values are obtained for all subjects. Then, the difference between the actual, obtained treatment EMG and the predicted value is obtained. This "difference" or "residual" score for each subject is then inserted into a standard computational 2 × 2 analysis of variance. One *df* is subtracted from the total *df* (and thus, of course, the error *df*) for each correlational effect so removed (obviously four in a 2 × 2 design). As far as I know, this is the only way to deal with this problem. It has to be used cautiously and with common sense, but can result in extracting experimental impacts which might otherwise be overlooked, lost or masked [personal communication, January 27, 1978].

In the interest of advancing on some of these important topics, I have asked Jeffrey A. Kadlac to comment further on these issues (personal communication, December 17, 1978).

Dr. Reuder's remarks are very thoughtful and valuable for our field. While I agree in principle with a critical attention to statistical assumptions and control of Type I error rates, my bias in practice is for parsimonious and cautiously liberal statistical methods. This bias stems from several considerations:

1. A number of empirical studies (e.g., Boneau, 1960; Bradley, 1964) have amply demonstrated that F and t tests are very robust with respect to violations of homogeneity of variance assumptions. This is especially true when the number of observations is equal across experimental conditions. Furthermore, F and t statistics are more versatile and powerful than their nonparametric counterparts (Anderson, 1961).

2. The problem that Dr. Reuder addresses is particular to within-subjects (repeated measures) designs. These designs, which are prevalent in psychophysiological research, may produce heterogeneity of covariance, the consequences of which are greater than for heterogeneity of variance. The problem is due to the mathematical fact that homogeneity of covariances is required in order for the ratio of mean squares to be distributed precisely as F. Box (1954) has shown that, all other things being equal, the F test will generally be positively biased when the covariances are heterogeneous.

3. A variety of ways have been proposed for detecting and dealing with the problems of heterogeneity of variance and covariance, but they all seem to introduce additional problems. Data transformations have been used successfully, but suitable transformations cannot always be found, and their use requires, of course, that our psychological inferences also be based upon the transformed data. Methods employing df corrections (e.g., Box, 1954) generally err in the direction of being either too conservative or too liberal and may not permit clear inferences. Techniques that use F tests of variance are, unlike F tests in ANOVA, strongly dependent on normality assumptions. Tests for nonadditivity (e.g., Tukey, 1949) cannot detect all forms of nonadditivity. And, finally, corrections that involve correlation calculations may be subject to most of the problems of correlational inference and are not altogether satisfactory. For one thing, they are prone to range effects; sample correlations may be artificially increased or decreased by changes in the range of manipulated variables. Second, correlations are strongly based on normal distribution assumptions; non-normal distribu-

tions of the dependent variable may limit the possible values that the correlation coefficient may attain. Third, and surely most important, the Pearson Product Moment correlation coefficient, r, is a measure of the linear relationship between variables and does not take into account the possibility that the true relationship may be nonlinear (for example, a U or inverted-U-shaped function). Thus, an exclusive focus on corrections for linear relationships may be in some cases misleading, and it may be argued that nonlinear corrections should also be routinely applied.

4. Statistical techniques are, of course, secondary to our primary responsibility of looking at and making inferences from our data. Statistics do not actually tell us whether a given effect is or is not present, as classical hypothesis-testing procedures would lead us to believe. Rather, they give us an indication of the relative likelihood that the apparent results (determined by close examination of the data) were obtained by chance. In conjunction with some fairly well accepted conventions (e.g., the .05 significance level) that establish criteria for the burden of proof, statistics lend a "seal of good housekeeping," as it were, to those effects we wish to claim are real. But there is nothing sacred about these decision criteria; they are conventions—nothing more, nothing less. The more serious errors in the literature involve experimental design and interpretation of substance, not simple determination of statistical significance. In the real world, very few null hypotheses are strictly true; it is the magnitude, direction, and practical significance of effects that are primarily open to question.

8.7
The Use of Computers
by Jeffrey A. Kadlac

Computers are an increasingly useful means of coping with the vast amounts of data collected in psychophysiological research. They can save considerable amounts of time and busy work involved in data collection, transformation, reduction, quantification, and analysis. But the costs are often dear in terms of initial effort to achieve a workable, accurate, and flexible system. These costs include programming, debugging, interfacing, and verification that the computer is doing the kinds of processing you seek.

Even after the initial expenditures of effort and money, a number of things may go wrong—and will, eventually. Programs will have to be periodically updated and generalized to handle a wider variety of experimental problems and data analyses. Electronic parts and interfaces may break down, sometimes in subtle ways that may be difficult to diagnose without knowledge of both programming and electronics. Each of these problems may be expensive (again in terms of time, effort, and/or money) to repair, so allowances should be made.

Perhaps the most serious problem in the use of computers in the laboratory is due to the fact that one is no longer in close contact with the raw data. Therefore, it is *imperative* that the output of data reduction and scoring programs be thoroughly tested for validity—that is, meticulously compared to the output obtained from hand scoring. Specific attention should be given to the possibility that the computer algorithms, which may be simple in essence, might somehow introduce systematic biases that affect experimental conclusions. In this effort, one should play the devil's advocate, making allowance for every conceivable situation. Ultimately, it may be best to do some routine trial-by-trial checking of the computer data to look for artifacts, even with a working system. The extent to which this is necessary or feasible, however, varies from situation to situation.

All of this is not to say that the computer is always an adversary. Indeed, one of the main benefits of computer analysis, in addition to the saving of considerable effort in the long run, lies in its ultimate objectivity. The computer does simply what we tell it to do. Thus it can avoid the often subtle biases that are always possible when we score data by hand—unless, of course, we unintentionally program such biases into the computer algorithms.

8.8
Troubleshooting

An advertisement for an employment agency could well state that "There is always a future in electronic maintenance," particularly in psychophysiological laboratories. There is, in fact, a widely held belief among psychophysiologists that for each there is a personal poltergeist who capriciously intervenes in his or her laboratory system at critical times. So many of the common "laws of experimentation" are especially appropriate to the psychophysiological laboratory ("anything that can go wrong will go wrong"; "everything goes wrong at one time"; "if several things can go wrong, the one that will go wrong is that which will do the most harm"; "if your lab seems to be going well, you have overlooked something"; and the like). The solution to apparatus problems is prevention; and prevention *can* be accomplished by developing a stable laboratory. There are so many good rules for building a laboratory (good soldering connections, cables well shielded and firmly placed low on the floor, an effective permanent grounding system) that we cannot go into them in any detail here. Instead, several thoughts about troubleshooting will be offered along with the general counsel that care in constructing the laboratory can sizably reduce the need to troubleshoot.

Once the experimenter has developed a stable laboratory, the read-out system should be monitored every time some system change is made, such as each time new equipment is brought in. Compulsive checking for the effects of any change will be worth the effort. The purpose is to make sure that the change has not altered normal recording. When checking out the laboratory system, there should be some electrical resistance placed between the electrodes. However, it is not always convenient, nor even desirable, to attach electrodes to a human for the purpose of monitoring signals from them while troubleshooting. A good substitute is a "dummy subject," a 10,000 ohm resistor, which may be placed between the electrodes. With the "dummy" resistance, the experimenter can then monitor a cathode ray oscilloscope for distorted or unwanted signals without using a live subject.

To locate the source of unwanted signals, one can search throughout the laboratory with the psychophysiologist's "magic wand." A "magic wand" can be easily constructed by placing a 10,000 ohm resistor between the single ended input to a CRO and the shielding conduit (grounded, of course) of the single-ended cable. By being placed on the end of a long cable connected to an oscilloscope that is set to a low-voltage scale (1 mv per division suffices), the resistor can be moved throughout the lab near pieces of equipment. In this way, stray signals become readily apparent on the CRO and, once detected, their source can be found and properly dealt with. Many strange signals at various frequencies can appear. In addition to those from 60-cycle power lines, interference from other equipment can ride in from other laboratories in the vicinity on AC or DC lines (we once spent 3 days tracing a 2000-Hz signal to the chemistry lab upstairs).

Although one can emphasize the prevention of difficulties, problems still appear when electrodes are being attached to a subject; moment-to-moment monitoring of the signals on a CRO may indicate that the bodily signal is not coming through or that the desired signal is partially attenuated by being superimposed on a 60-cycle signal. At that point, the experimenter needs to discover and correct the problem very rapidly in order to "save the data." If it is a stable, well constructed laboratory, broken connections are an unlikely source of the problem, so attention can be turned to higher probability sources. There might be poor contact between the electrode and the skin surface, but a break in the electrode lead itself is not frequent. One might diagnose such problems by placing each lead of an ohmmeter on the surface of each of the two electrodes respectively in order to measure interelectrode resistance. The rule of thumb is that resistance in excess of 10,000 ohms may prevent the desired bodily signals from adequately entering the amplifiers. The experimenter could then use the ohmmeter to run a continuity check to ensure there is no break in the electrode leads. If the electrodes are in satisfactory condition, they may be removed and then replaced after further massaging of the skin to reduce cutaneous resistance. Incidentally, although it is typical to measure resistance with an ohmmeter, a measure of impedance (with an Electrode Impedance Tester) is actually preferable for biphasic signals like EMG and EEG. To be absolutely correct, impedance is the proper measure for transient (AC) types of signals such as EMG and EEG, whereas resistance is the measure appropriate for DC types of signals. Furthermore, measuring resistance with an ohmmeter might produce a slight, but harmless, shock for the subject, whereas shocks are not possible with the impedance tester.

Another possible problem that can appear while preparing the subject is that there are conductive paths of detergent, water, or electrode paste between two placements on the skin; these could virtually eliminate useful EMG signals from the subject.

Problems like these with electrodes would appear in only one channel, whereas trouble in all channels would indicate a more general problem (poor subject ground, extraneous noise, etc.). Extraneous noise may come from a piece of equipment that has been overloaded or perhaps from some change in the environment. An extremely accomplished psychophysiologist in my acquaintance had such an environmental problem that was caused by a new TV station a mile from his laboratory. A TV station emits a high-frequency signal that can penetrate inexpensive shielding like copper mesh; in his case, the signal would wax and wane at 60 cycles per second (a "sync. signal"), appearing in the records as 60 Hz, yet not emanating from a power line. Unfortunately, the psychophysiologist never did solve this problem.

8.9
Laboratory Safety

Shock hazard to subjects and experimenters, the primary laboratory danger, is a function of the amount of current that flows through the body. To gain some perspective, a current less than 1 milliamp is readily perceptible, whereas 10 to 100 milliamps can cause pain, burns, and tetanus of the involved musculature. Currents in excess of 100 milliamps are likely to cause cardiac and respiratory arrest. Shock hazards exist to the subject because the subject is grounded by a special electrode; hence, just as when one is in the bathtub, any contact with a power line could cause electrical current to be conducted through the body with potentially fatal consequences.

The best protection is never to bring 110 or 220 AC power lines into the subject room and never to use any equipment in the subject room that requires such a power source. (As noted earlier, another argument against bringing electrical equipment into the subject room is that the equipment is a source of electromagnetic transmission that produces undesired noise.) If, however, it *is* necessary to bring AC-operated equipment into the subject room, it is critical that a grounded subject not be allowed to touch that equipment, as it may be conducting leakage currents from the lower line that activates it. Leakage currents are typically small, and their presence is not commonly recognized. I once asked a manufacturer's representative if there was an electrical current on the surface of my electric typewriter. When he answered "No," we were both surprised when I measured a small but noticeable leakage current. Such currents can range from well below threshold to fatal levels, depending on various conditions.

In the case of electrodes inserted beneath the skin, the danger is easily fatal. When using surface electrodes, the danger of shock to the subject is less, but still present. With inserted electrodes, a safety standard is to assure that there is less than 5 one-millionths of an ampere flow through the subject. There have been reports of patients in hospital beds with implanted electrodes being electrocuted by turning on their bedside lamp—the leakage current on the lamp was sufficient to be fatal.

Methods of eliminating shock hazards include use of only battery-operated equipment in the vicinity of the subject and careful grounding of any necessary line-operated equipment that the subject could conceivably touch. Each piece of apparatus should be grounded separately to the common point at which the subject's ground wire connects (see Fig. 18). This common point should be connected to the primary laboratory ground cable. Whenever possible, avoid using a grounded outlet for the ground system, because these become unsafe with age and corrosion. Likewise, avoid having two separate ground systems within the reach of the subject, for there can exist considerable voltages and currents between the two ground systems. With proper grounding in the subject's vicinity, safety even in the event of equipment malfunction can be assured.

Small shocks can occur in the laboratory through a variety of unusual circumstances. We have mentioned one, merely testing electrode resistance with an ohmmeter. Even such small shocks are undesirable, because they can provide a bad experimental set for the subject. To keep subjects' expectations positive, it is advisable never to use intentional shock in a psychophysiological lab; this precaution could help prevent the arousal of gruesome rumors about the lab that can make it difficult to attract subjects, who already have a tendency to think that all the electrical equipment means that shock is in store for them. Although we have concentrated on shock hazards to the subject, the principles apply equally to the experimenter; the difference is that we know the subject is grounded. But, if the experimenter should become momentarily grounded by accidentally touching a grounding cable, there are many ways in which the experimenter, too, can be shocked (e.g., coming into contact with excessive leakage current on an oscilloscope, or with an instrument that has an electrical short).

8.10
Evaluation of the Laboratory

The primary criterion for judging the technical capabilities of the laboratory is whether or not a faithful recording of the event of interest has been achieved. To assess the fidelity of a laboratory system, one can enter signals with known characteristics into the electrodes. Various parameters of the input signal can then be compared with the output signal on the read-out system. A sample of several different types of waveforms ideally should be entered into the laboratory system, so that possible distortions can be checked. A sine wave is most typically generated for this purpose, but other useful waves that can be entered into the system are square waves, pulses, triangular waves, and sawtoothed waves. Signal-generating instruments that yield a variety of waveforms are available as standard equipment from manufacturers. Guld, Rosenfalck, and Willison (1970) suggested a function generator (e.g., Wavetek, Model 112) to produce signals resembling various action potentials. Such signals, varying in duration and slope and triggered at regular and irregular intervals, provide more extensive tests of fidelity than a mere sine or square wave. Several waveforms that they studied have been found to be helpful in detecting defects and limitations in the system tested.

For a detailed discussion of principles of assessing laboratory fidelity, the reader is referred to Geddes and Baker (1968). A brief summary of the specific criteria that they offer for positively evaluating a laboratory system follows:

1. *Amplitude linearity*—the output amplitude of the system should be directly proportional to the input amplitude.
2. *Adequate bandwidth*—the frequency range specified by the amplifiers should be adequate to allow the recording of a true amplitude for the covert events being studied. Adequate bandwidth provides the ability of the system to follow rapid and slow changes in the bodily event that is being sensed.
3. *Phase linearity*—there should be an absence of phase distortion.

One test for phase distortion is to superimpose a constant signal on a continuous known signal (e.g., a notch can be placed in the peak of a sine wave); the output of the known signal can then be observed to determine whether the position of the constant signal (e.g., the notch) varies from its known input position.

In addition to its use for testing the fidelity of the laboratory system, a signal generator can be used for calibration purposes. For calibrating measurements of covert processes, it is important to be able to generate signals of varying amplitude, particularly very low voltage signals down to the 1 μv level. There are also calibration instruments that can vary output impedance and provide common mode signals and variable frequencies.[10]

The input signal with known characteristics that is applied for testing laboratory fidelity and for calibration purposes can be applied directly to the electrodes (or transducer) to be amplified and recorded on the read-out system. Alternatively, it can be switched into each channel at some point after the electrodes and prior to the amplifiers; this is an especially effective way to enter a known calibration signal at the beginning of each experimental session or at selected times thereafter. Most often the calibration command switch is manually controlled. A more elegant calibration system can be

---

[10]Whereas a standard instrument like a function generator, a signal generator, or a microvolter may be purchased from a manufacturer, the experimenter might wish instead to construct one. Sheatz (1972) presented a circuit that can be used to construct a differential microvolt signal generator that is suitable for this purpose.

designed to automatically enter a calibrating signal whenever recording is initiated. Automatic calibration systems can also be programmed to emit calibration signals at selected times during recording and to shut down automatically so that only calibration signals of limited duration are emitted. One can even program a computer to compare parameters of the output signal with those of the input signal by storing standard signals in the computer's memory.

8.11
Conclusion

Although complex laboratory equipment is necessary for the study of covert processes, the laboratory system should still be kept as simple as possible. A primary conclusion is that we should have as little apparatus as is reasonably possible and should never develop equipment that is more complicated than necessary to get the job done. We must be wary of the pitfalls that befall researchers who become so enamored with apparatus construction, computer programming, statistical analysis, and the like that they needlessly complicate their tasks and sometimes even lose sight of their original research goals. In short, everything else being equal, the simpler the laboratory system, the more efficiently the research can be conducted.

Another general principle that should guide the psychophysiologist is that in the last analysis, the psychophysiologist has to make his or her own decisions about how to best accomplish individual purposes in his or her own laboratory. Although it is advisable to study the many valuable references on psychophysiological and electronic techniques, and although experts can offer much general advice, such information does not necessarily apply in the unique situation of any individual psychophysiological laboratory.[11] A general procedure for the psychophysiologist is to try out a number of different types of supplies and equipment (often manufacturers furnish apparatus on trial) and keep records of performance under a variety of

-----

[11]Recall Einstein's analogous comment that a mathematician can tell a scientist a lot of things, but seldom what one needs to know at any given time.

conditions, eventually selecting those that provide relatively good recording under the existing laboratory conditions. For example, one should try several different kinds of electrodes, jellies, and pastes and evaluate several different methods of application of these (styrofoam pads, tape, etc.). Such experiences establish a sound basis for future standard laboratory procedures.

Relatively simple and inexpensive items often are equal or superior to more complex and expensive ones. For example, over the years we have tried out a large number of different kinds of electrodes and have concluded that the relatively inexpensive electrodes manufactured by Grass Instruments are completely satisfactory. They provide excellent recordings and remain usable for years, compared to some that must be discarded immediately, or after several months.

In this section, we have reviewed various technical considerations for studying covert processes. More advanced and detailed sources of information about equipment and methodology include the following: Camishion (1964), Cohen and Brumlik (1968), Fogel and George (1967), Fox and Rosenfeld (1973), Geddes (1972), Geddes and Baker (1968), Greenfield and Sternback (1972), Grings (1954), Guld et al. (1970), Levine (1968), Malmstadt, Enke, and Toren (1963), Myers (1973), Sidowski (1966), Suprynowicz (1966), Thompson and Patterson (1973), Venables and Martin (1967), Wilkinson, Herbert, and Branton (1973), Yanof (1973), and Zimmer and Krusberg (1966).

In addition, two issues of *American Psychologist* (March 1969 and March 1975) have been devoted to instrumentation in psychology. Articles in the 1969 issue that are of direct interest for the study of covert processes are those by White on evoked cortical responses, by Vladimirov and Homskaya on eye recording, by Ax and by Johnson and Naitoh on general instrumentation, and by Mackay on telemetry; also, an article by Haith gives an application of infrared television to the study of ocular behavior in the human infant.

In the 1975 issue, the psychophysiologist might pay special attention to the use of biomedical telemetry (Sandler, McCutcheon, Fryer, Rositano, Westbrook, and Haro), cardiovascular psychophysiology (Obrist, Gaebelein, and Langer), blood-pressure monitoring (Krausman), eye-movement recording (Monty; Young and Sheena), "alpha machines" (Schwitzgebel and Rugh), biofeedback instrumentation (Paskewitz), microwaves (Justesen), and the measurement of genital responses (Geer). Both issues also consider the general use of computers, the 1975 issue giving the greater coverage because of the sizable advances in computer technology (especially solid-state electronics and packaging) that have allowed the development of the small, inexpensive computer. Computers have numerous, extremely valuable applications in the psychophysiology laboratory, particularly for data reduction and stimulus control. Psychophysiological data probably pose the most difficult analysis problems of any that psychologists face. It is not unusual for many miles of "squiggles" to be recorded in a days work, making it difficult and time-consuming to define a response. However, computers can perform this task. For example, McGuigan and Pavek (1972) programmed a computer to search for response outputs from the various electrode placements on their subjects. The computer continuously computed the mean and standard deviation of the analog signals; when an amplitude was identified that exceeded a certain number of standard deviations from the mean, a response was defined, and the latency, duration, and amplitude of the response were printed out. With this method, they found a most interesting eye response that would not have been detected by visual means alone (Figs. 4 and 5).

A final source of information about equipment is the *Handbook of Engineering in Medicine and Biology* by Fleming and Feinberg (1975). Although generally concerned with medical and other issues not directly relevant, it does contain some pertinent information about transducers, electrodes, amplifiers, analysis of ECGs and EEGs, and characteristics (including electrical characteristics) of bodily signals.

A THEORETICAL FRAMEWORK FOR PSYCHOPHYSIOLOGICALLY MEASURED COVERT PROCESSES

In Part 1, we specified as our goal the understanding of behavior, both overt and covert. The traditional psychological approach to achieve this goal has been to develop stimulus–response laws, including the hypothesization of a variety of logical constructs. The psychologist, working strictly at the level of observable external stimuli and overt responses has thus been hampered by inability to do more than indirectly infer the nature of the processes intervening between the S and the R. More recently, the knowledge explosion within the area of psychophysiology is indicative of attempts to fill those gaps between S and R through the direct measurement of covert processes.

An illustrative methodology for directly studying such hypothesized events is in the work of McGuigan and Boness (1975), entitled "What Happens Between an External Stimulus and an Overt Response." In Fig. 31, we see a sample of their psychophysiologically recorded events, and in Fig. 32, we see a plot of the temporal relationships among those events.

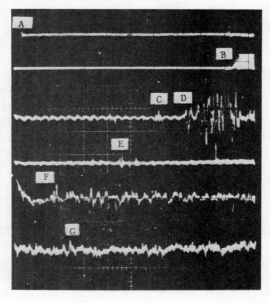

FIG. 31. Sample tracings illustrative of the major findings. *A:* blank indicates stimulus presentation. *B:* overt response. *C:* isolated covert reaction in the active limb. *D:* onset of the covert response in the active limb that builds up to the overt response that produces *B. E:* isolated covert response in the passive limb. *F:* covert response in the tongue. *G:* covert response in the eye. Amplitude is 50 μv per centimeter except for the tongue, which is 100 μv per division. Each horizontal centimeter is 50 msec.

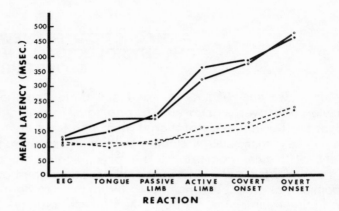

FIG. 32. Mean latency of the earliest identified reaction for each bodily region. The top two traces are for choice reaction time; the lower two traces are for simple reaction time. Filled circles are for linguistic stimuli; unfilled circles are for nonlinguistic stimuli.

The psychophysiologist's approach has had short-comings just as the classical behavioral approach, but for a different reason (viz., because of the lack of a guiding theoretical framework for the empirical measurement of psychophysiological phenomena). What we have learned through psychophysiological measurement has been initiated primarily by basic, low-level, and limited empirical hypotheses rather than by more general, higher-level statements containing theoretical constructs. By wedding the behavioristic and psychophysiological approaches, efforts within both domains should be enhanced through mutually facilitating techniques, approaches, and findings. The purpose in this concluding section, therefore, is to attempt to interweave behaviorism and psychophysiology.

We have assumed that it is impossible to understand any behavioral unit in isolation from the rest of the body and have followed a model of complex interactions of the various bodily systems in order to comprehend cognitive functioning. Steps in developing a formal theory of covert processes require three hypothetical constructs and their interrelationships, as in Fig. 33. These three constructs, the covert oral response (r_O), the covert nonoral response ($r_{\dot{O}}$), and the covert neurophysiological reaction (ρ_N) may be evoked by external linguistic stimuli (S_L). The enormously complex interactions among these three classes of events are summarized by single arrows, indicating that each class of reaction sets off instances of every other class. The ongoing interactions of these three classes of events result in an overt response (R_L) that is the termination of this behavioral unit.[12]

At a theoretical level, the covert response has traditionally been considered a hypothetical construct (X) defined according to classical procedures such as those employed by Hull (1943) or by Tolman (1932). Hypothetical constructs are defined by means of functional relationships between external stimuli (S) that anchor them on the antecedent side and overt responses (R) that anchor them on the consequent side [hence, the paradigm $S-(X)-R$]. For example, Hull's covert fractional anticipatory goal response (r_G) was defined by externally observable stimuli and responses according to the functional relationships specified by the paradigm: $S-r_G-s_G-R$. Essentially the same approach to theoretical covert reactions has been used by many others (McGuigan, 1978).

Although behavioristic paradigms for anchoring constructs of covert processes have been quite successfully employed—the outstanding success of Osgood and his colleagues (e.g., Osgood & Hoosain, 1974) in measuring meaning (r_M) through such techniques as the semantic differential is an excellent example—we seek to compliment this classical approach by means of psychophysiological techniques. In this regard, we note that hypothetical constructs are considered to have "reality status" and thus are potentially observable (as distinguished from intervening variables, MacCorquodale & Meehl, 1948). The three major classes of covert processes (covert oral responses, covert nonoral responses, and covert neurophysiological processes) can thus also be empirically anchored directly through the psychophysiological methods specified in Table 1. Figure 34

---

[12]The question as to how different classes of stimulus events function to produce differences in consequent covert and overt reactions is important. In classical cognitive psychology, linguistic stimuli and linguistic responses have been given a priority status, although nonverbal thought has not been neglected at all. Hence, whereas S_L in Fig. 33 represents linguistic information input, a similar paradigm could be proposed for nonlinguistic information input; and there would be additional interactions in a more complex paradigm between verbal and nonverbal thought processes, perhaps involving hemispheric interactions.

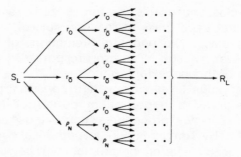

FIG. 33. Representation of three classes of hypothetical constructs: covert oral responses (r_O), covert nonoral responses ($r_{\bar{O}}$), and covert neurophysiological processes (ρ_N). Complex interactions are represented here with arrows, although the representation of them as neuromuscular circuit components in Fig. 35 is more realistic.

graphically illustrates this approach in which hypothetical constructs that intervene between external stimuli and overt responses are operationally defined in terms of the techniques of electromyography, electroencephalography, electro-oculography, etc. (Table 1). We may thus note that the three hypothetical constructs (ρ_N, r_O, and $r_{\bar{O}}$) intervening between the external linguistic stimulus (S_L) and the overt linguistic response (R_L) are directly tied to their psychophysiological data bases as well as to their indirect data bases (S_L and R_L). Reichenbach (1932) referred to this relationship between the formal constructs and the data level as that of a coordinating definition; Northrop (1948) identified the relationship as an epistemic correlation.

In considering how the various bodily systems represented by the constructs of covert oral behavior, covert nonoral behavior, and neurophysiological reactions interact, we can consider the neuromuscular information-processing model represented in Fig. 35. The basic notion is that the various cognitive phenomena with which psychology has dealt over the years occur when there is selective activation of the composite circuits represented in Fig. 35. Perceptions, thoughts, ideas, images, hallucinations, dreams, or whatever, by this model, are common-sense terms denoting cognitive events produced during internal information processing when various of these circuits are activated.

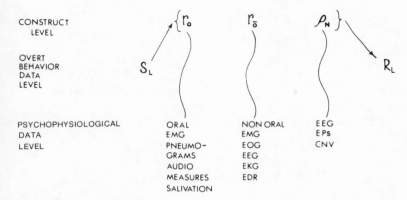

FIG. 34. Three hypothetical constructs directly measured through psychophysiological methods.

Elsewhere we have detailed some of the abundant anatomical and physiological evidence about these specific circuits (loops) between a wide variety of peripheral mechanisms and the brain (McGuigan, 1978). The first class of circuit (designated Ia) occurs when stimuli excite receptors, whereupon afferent neural impulses evoke brain events that result in efferent impulses back to the receptor. Such loops must reverberate for some time following stimulus reception. There is also the probability of extra-CNS loops between receptors and other peripheral mechanisms, like the receptor–speech muscle–brain circuits designated by the symbols Ib and Ib'. The second general class of circuit (which would function for sensory integration—for integrating the two images from the eyes, for example) would consist strictly of intracerebral loops (II). These may include circuits between the cortex and subcortical regions (Penfield, 1969) as well as complex transcortical loops, such as Hebb's (1949) cell assemblies. The third class of circuit involves cerebral–speech muscle activity (IIIa) and cerebral–somatic muscle activity (IIIb). Hence, when external linguistic stimuli impinge on the organism, the first class of circuit Ib and Ib' is activated, following which sensory integration (for separate input from the two eyes, the two ears, etc.) occurs when circuit class II reverberates. Simultaneously, there is skeletal speech–muscle and nonspeech–muscle activity through the circuit classes

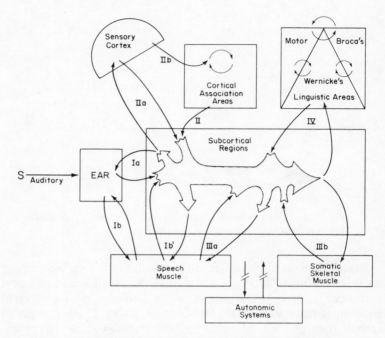

FIG. 35.   A neuromuscular circuit model for internal information processing.

IIIa and IIIb. These latter circuits are important for the generation of linguistic codes that are then transmitted to and from the linguistic regions of the brain for lexical–semantic processing. It is during this latter stage (circuit class IV) that meaningful perception (interpretation) of the external stimuli occurs. A rather detailed consideration of how this internal information processing model may be used to explicate the "higher mental processes" may be found in Chapters 9 and 10 of McGuigan (1978). Here, we merely mention this neuromuscular circuit model for heuristic value in guiding our psychophysiological laboratory research: The task for the cognitive psychophysiologist is to measure components of these neuromuscular circuits and to temporally relate those measured events to trace out the circuits that are critical during cognitive functioning, as in Fig. 36. In discussing this figure, McGuigan and Pavek (1972) state that:

Complex feedback loops might function to integrate the speech musculature (lips, tongue, etc.) with the speech regions of the brain, and with the eye, related perhaps to a covert nod or shake of the head (indicated by the response in the neck region). Differential linguistic patterns should be identifiable at this instant, as in the case of duration of eye response [Figs. 4 and 5]. Concomitant with this intraperipheral and interperipheral and central integration in which a YES–NO decision is reached [Fig. 36], and part of the almost simultaneous running off of these feedback loops, a "command" is issued to the passive arm that is inhibitory in nature—it may be that the active arm can only overtly respond once the passive arm is commanded to "not respond" (hence, a more rapid response in the passive arm relative to that in the active arm).... Such an inhibitory response, involving as it does the skeletal musculature, might be the behavioral counterpart of inhibitory neural activity, as reported by Hernández-Peón, Scherrer, and Jouvet (1956). Finally, continuing this line of speculation, after the complex decision (YES or NO) was made, the

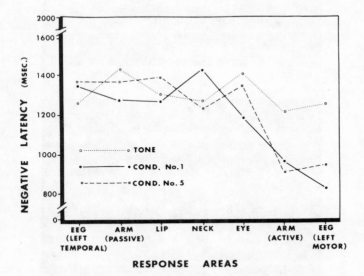

FIG. 36. Relative mean latencies of responses identified in various bodily regions. (The higher the data point on the vertical scale, the earlier the response following stimulus termination.)

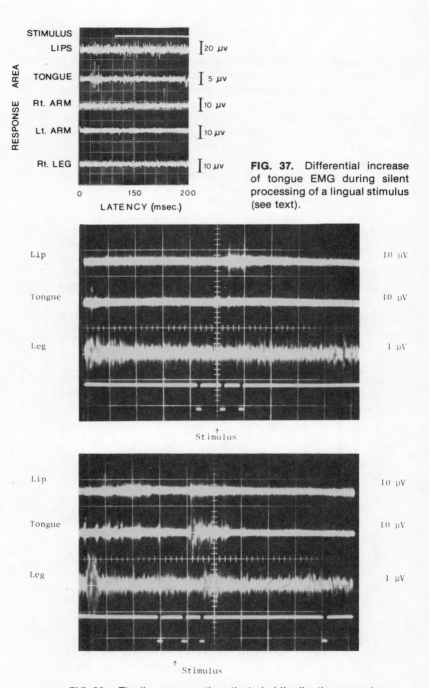

FIG. 37. Differential increase of tongue EMG during silent processing of a lingual stimulus (see text).

FIG. 38. The lips are covertly activated while silently processing bilabial verbal material (above), as the tongue is when processing lingual verbal material (lower) (see text).

dominant motor cortex was uniquely activated, "commanding" the overt response to be made in the active arm [McGuigan & Pavek, 1972, p. 244].

Other instances of differential muscle responding are illustrated in Figs. 37, 38, and 39. In Fig. 37, we note the heightened tongue EMG during the silent processing of lingual verbal material, which when spoken overtly requires major lingual (tongue) activity. Note the quiescent lips, which are activated during the silent processing of bilabial (not lingual) verbal material (McGuigan & Winstead, 1974). The lips and tongue are similarly differentially activated during presentation of stimuli for memorization in a short-term memory paradigm, as we found in a preliminary study by Thorsheim, Davis, and McGuigan (Fig. 38). A final illustration is the activation of a secretary's preferred arm during compressed speech comprehension (Fig. 39). By employing all of the psychophysiological variables specified in Table 1 (and new ones, too), we should make progress toward the direct measurement of the various cognitive events that are of primary concern to the psychologist and related scientists.

A summary of the various kinds of circuits and their functioning is presented in Fig. 40. There we note that complex

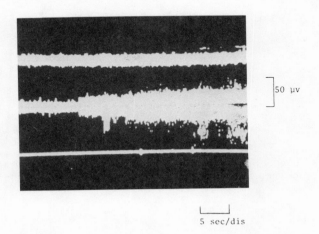

50 μv

5 sec/dis

FIG. 39. During compressed speech perception, a secretary proficient in shorthand reported that she was covertly writing the speech as if it were dictated. Note the increased activity in the preferred arm (second trace) with little change in the lips (top) or leg (lower).

interactions between the speech muscle and central nervous system occur in the generation of the type of linguistic code referred to as a *phonetic code* and in those nonoral skeletal muscle components that function in the generation of the type of linguistic code referred to as an *allographic code* (as detailed in McGuigan, 1978). We also have considered neuromuscular circuits that function during nonverbal thought by generating what we have referred to as a *referent level code.* And, finally, there are circuits involving the autonomic system for adding emotional tone to our mental activity. In conjunction, these various volleys are transmitted to and from their appropriate regions of the brain (the verbal coding to and from the linguistic regions for lexical–semantic processing, the nonverbal coding perhaps to selected regions of the minor hemisphere for nonlinguistic processing, and the autonomic systems with the subcortical regions of the brain for emotional processing).

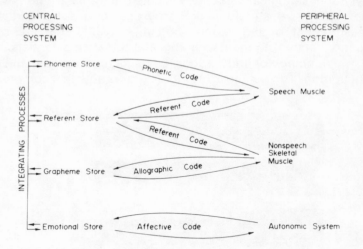

FIG. 40. Representation of possible peripheral–central processing interactions and corresponding neuromuscular codes.

Note #1:
Telemetry

In place of leads from the electrodes going directly into the amplifiers, the electrode signals may be led by very short wires into a radio-type transmitter that is attached to the subject. The transmitter (quite small, often about the size of the thumb) may then be used to send any of a variety of psychophysiological signals by *telemetry* to a receiver that directs the signals into the amplifier.

The technique of telemetry is probably more applicable when the subject is mobile or a long distance away from the amplifiers and recording systems (as when monitoring astronauts) than when the subject is stationary and quiet (as in the study of covert processes). But telemetry may be valuable (though more expensive) for some purposes, and it does eliminate bothersome electrode leads into the amplifiers. If telemetry is used in a shielded laboratory, the radio signal obviously could not be transmitted through the shielded walls of the subject room to the amplifier in the apparatus room. To solve this problem, one could place an aerial through the shielded wall with one end penetrating the subject room (to receive the signal) and the other end penetrating the equipment room, where a cable conducts the signal directly into the amplifier. This solution requires that the aerial be insulated as it passes through the wall so that the signal of interest is not conducted into the shielding.

For further information on telemetry, consult Brown, Edge, and Horn (1971), Caceres and Cooper (1968), Kimmich and Vos (1972) and Mackay (1970).

Note #2:
Operational Amplifiers and
the Use of Negative Feedback

Briefly, consider an amplifier with an input, an output, and a loop from the output back to the input that contains a gain network (β). According to the classical equation developed by

Black (1934), with an amplification factor of A, the gain (G) of this system is:

$$G = A \left(\frac{1}{1 - A\beta} \right)$$

The system β provides a way of reducing voltage, such as what one can do with a voltage divider. Consequently, the amplification factor (A) is modified by the factor $[1/(1 - A\beta)]$. If the system (β) reduces voltage sufficiently for the factor $[1/(1 - A\beta)]$ to have absolute value less than 1, the feedback from the output to the input of the amplifier is classified as negative; hence, the system gain (G) is reduced relative to what it would have been with the amplifier alone (A); that is, the loop from the output of the amplifier back to the input, containing as it does the system β, can reduce the output voltage itself by dividing that voltage and entering but a portion of it again into the input stage. In short, negative feedback occurs when the voltage from the output subtracts from the input voltage.

Let us illustrate by means of an example. Suppose that the system (β) reduces the output voltage of the amplifier to 10% of its standard value. In this instance, it can be shown by the Black equation that the addition of 10% negative feedback would reduce an amplifier gain of 1000 to 9.9. Now suppose that amplifier tube aging, operating voltage, etc., decreases the amplification factor (A) from 1000 to 900. With 10% negative feedback, there would be a reduction in the total system gain of only .1% (i.e., from 9.90 to 9.89). Even with a decrease in amplifier gain (A) of 90%, the overall system gain would be reduced by only 8.2% (i.e., from 9.90 to 9.09). Negative feedback thus stabilizes the entire system gain, because decreases in system gain (G) are minimal with the loop system (β) relative to amplifier gain (A) without (β). To show how this increase in system gain stability due to negative feedback can be used to construct operational amplifiers with extremely large gain factors, consider a loop gain ($A\beta$) that is quite large (much greater than 1); in this event, the 1 in the denominator of the Black equation becomes relatively unimportant and can be ignored. The system gain then changes from:

$$G = \frac{A}{1 - A\beta}$$

to

$$G = \frac{A}{-A\beta} = \frac{1}{-\beta}$$

Hence, when the loop gain ($A\beta$) is quite large, the system gain is essentially a function of the characteristics of the feedback network and is independent of the amplifier gain (A). Operational amplifiers can use this principle to develop extremely high gains by special construction of the feedback loop (viz., by varying the ratio of a resistor in the input circuit prior to the amplifier and the resistor placed in the feedback loop).

To illustrate how negative feedback can reduce noise and distortion arising within the amplifier, consider an amplifier that has two amplification Stages, A_1 and A_2, such that the input signal is amplified successively in each stage by factors A_1 and A_2. Thus the total amplification factor (A) is equal to the product of that for each stage (viz., $A_1 \times A_2$). If noise is introduced within the amplifier between the two stages, the noise is added to the output of Stage A_1 and therefore to the input of Stage A_2. It can be mathematically shown (Geddes & Baker, 1968, p. 363) that the noise thus introduced is reduced through negative feedback (by the factor $1/A_1$); that is, negative feedback allows a noise-free gain to enter ahead of the point at which noise enters the amplifier, allowing the noise to be reduced in the output of the operational amplifier in inverse proportion to the gain of the first amplifier Stage A_1. In short, in this application of the negative feedback principle, noise that enters at the input (prior to Stage A_1) is not reduced, but noise entering within the amplifier (after Stage A_1) is reduced.

Note #3:
Procedure for Computing Response Voltage at the Subject

Measurements reported are, of course, in terms of amplitude and frequency values as they are generated at the subject (in contrast to meaningless values that might be measured after amplification). Hence, to measure response amplitude in terms of voltage at the subject, one should measure the height of the tracing on an oscilloscope, using the amplitude setting on the scope to determine the voltage per centimeter. One then notes the amplification used for that particular measurement (perhaps X10,000, X100,000, or X1,000,000). The voltage at the subject is then determined by dividing the amplitude measured on the oscilloscope by the amplification factor. For example, if the scope setting was 1 volt per centimeter, and the measured amplitude of the tracing on the scope was two volts (i.e., 2 cm high), and the channel amplification was X10,000, the computation would be:

$$\text{Subject voltage} = \frac{2 \text{ volts}}{10,000} = \frac{2,000,000 \ \mu v}{10,000} = 200 \ \mu v$$

Note #4:
Electrode Placement Procedure

There are a variety of techniques for attaching electrodes to a subject, the following being one effective procedure. The immediate area of the skin may be cleaned with a detergent such as PhisoHex or possibly Brasivol, which is more effective (but more harsh) in abrading the hard, high-resistance dead cells of the outer layers of the skin. Next, the jelly (such as Grass Electrojelly, Epi-Gel, etc.) should be rubbed on the skin for about 1 minute, with less rubbing time when attaching electrodes to the face (perhaps a maximum of 30 sec). The standard procedure is to massage the skin until it becomes slightly pink, but we have especially avoided this procedure (and Brasivol) for face electrodes. A greater amount of massaging needs to be done for the arms and the legs.

A wet glue foam pad such as that produced by Minnesota Mining and Manufacturing may be cut into small squares on which the back of the electrode may be attached to the glue substance. The electrode cup may then be filled (but not overflowing) with electrode jelly and the electrode placed on the prepared spot, the pad attaching the electrode to the skin; sometimes tape over the pad further secures the pad and the electrode under it to the skin. It is a good practice to prepare the skin for one electrode placement at a time only, as the experimenter may otherwise forget exactly where the skin was prepared.

In removing the electrode from the skin, one merely removes the foam pad. The electrode should then be removed from the pad by holding the electric cup, *not the wire.* Blot the skin to remove excess electrode jelly. The subject should then wash the electrode jelly from the skin on conclusion of the experiment. Electrodes may be placed in a glass of warm water and cleaned with a Q-tip.

For tongue electrodes that are held on by suction, one should make sure that the suction is off before removing the electrodes from the mouth (they should not be pulled off as they will merely fall off when the vacuum source is terminated). The tongue electrodes should be dipped in soapy water, then in distilled water, and placed in a dental disinfectant (e.g., Cetylcide) for about 5 minutes. Then they should be dried prior to use with the next subject.

The experimenter should never directly touch any electrode prior to placement on a subject, especially those that are to be placed within the mouth; rather, electrodes should be handled indirectly through the wires leading to them.

When leaving the laboratory, it is good practice to check to make sure that all electrodes are cleaned and that tops are placed back on the electrode jellies and bottles. Finally, make sure that the lab is neat and prepared for the next usage.

Note #5:
Procedure Sheet for a
Psychophysiology Laboratory

There are an infinite number of errors that can be made in the day-to-day conduct of a psychophysiological laboratory. To reduce the frequency of such errors (total elimination seems impossible), the experimenter may wish to construct a step-by-step check-off sheet to be used by all personnel conducting research in the laboratory. Any given check-off sheet would have to be modified for each laboratory, but one reasonably effective sheet is reproduced in Fig. 41 on the following pages.

FIG. 41. A sample procedure sheet for a psychophysiology laboratory.

Experiment Code Name:_____Date:_____

Group #:_____Subject #:_____

Condition:_____

Subject's Name:_____Experimenters:_____

Electrode Placement	Amplifier Settings		
		FILTER CUTOFF (Hz)	
Channel	Gain	Low	High
1			
2			
3			
4			
5			
6			
7			
8			

Data Tape Recording Speed:_____(inches/sec)

Footage Counter: Start at_____

End of experimental data at:_____

FIG. 41. *(continued)*

BEFORE SESSION DO THE FOLLOWING (Initial each item as it is accomplished):

Turn on:

_____ Main power

_____ Amplifier power on

_____ All scopes

_____ Data tape recorder on

_____ Check relaxation tape

_____ Intercom on

_____ Check all supplies

_____ Check for clean electrodes, especially tongue electrodes, which should be sterilized with Cetylcide, rinsed in distilled water, and dried

Slide Projector (If used):

_____ Power to slide projector

_____ Slide order for session

_____ Slide tray to beginning

_____ Any signal triggers (voice, photo cells)

Record Audio Identification on Data Tape of:

_____ Calibration data recorded

_____ Audio-recorder channel of data tape recorder

_____ Experiment (give title)

_____ Date

_____ Time

_____ Group # and Condition

_____ Subject #

_____ S's name

_____ E's names

_____ Channel identifications

FIG. 41. *(continued)*

DURING SESSION DO THE FOLLOWING:

____ Meet S, explain general procedures ("sensor," etc.)

____ Monitor each channel as electrodes are being connected for good signal.

____ Prepare to turn on vacuum punp for tongue electrodes when requested.

____ Ask S if "that will be O.K. with you" (informed consent)

____ Connect all electrodes except tongue

____ Turn on # Tape Recorder (press "PLAY" and "RECORD" simultaneously)

____ Play relaxation tape to establish a low baseline.

____ At end of relaxation tape, start experimental conditions

AFTER SESSION DO THE FOLLOWING:

____ Shut off vacuum for tongue electrodes

____ Return slide projector and audio tape recorders to beginning if used

____ Check specific gravity of each cell of 12 V storage batteries

____ Connect charger if needed

____ Rewind relaxation tape

____ Shut off apparatus if next session not soon

____ Debrief subject!

____ Swish tongue electrodes in Cetylcide, rinse in distilled H_2O, hang to dry

____ Thoroughly cleanse other electrodes in warm water

____ Check supplies

____ Restore covers to electrode pastes

____ Shut off data tape recorder

____ Shut off voice recorder

____ Record footage counter

____ Turn off scopes

____ Check for sufficient tape for next session, or erase a new tape for it, using only tapes authorized for erasure

FIG. 41. *(continued)*

_____ Meet with colleagues to discuss any items that have come up during session, and review time and date of next session

_____ Place this sheet and any data in your code name file

_____ Doublecheck this procedure sheet to ensure accuracy

11
ACRONYMS

AEP	Average evoked potentials	MAP	Muscle action potential (see EMG)
AER	Auditory evoked reaction	MP	Motor potential
BCD	Binary coded decimal	RP	Readiness potential
CNS	Central nervous system	SEP	Somatic evoked potential
CNV	Contingent negative variation	SER	Somatic evoked reaction
cps	Cycles per second (see Hz, preferred)	SPS	Steady potential shifts
CRO	Cathode ray oscilloscope	VEP	Visual evoked potential
CRT	Cathode ray tube	VER	Visual evoked reaction
EAP	Eye artifact potentials	r_G	Hull's fractional antedating goal reaction
ECG	Electrocardiogram (see EKG)	r_M	Osgood's meaning reaction ("response")
EEG	Electroencephalogram	R_L	Overt linguistic response
EKG	Electrocardiogram	r_L	Covert linguistic response
EMG	Electromyogram	r_O	Covert oral response
EOG	Electro-oculogram	$r_{\bar{o}}$	Covert nonoral response
EP	Evoked potentials	s_L	Internal linguistic stimulus
ERG	Electroretinogram	S_L	External linguistic stimulus
ERP	Event-related potentials		
GSR	Galvanic skin response		
Hz	Hertz (cps, cycles per second)		

GLOSSARY

Action potential: A localized electrical change in membrane permeability that is propagated along a neuron or muscle fiber (MAP).

Afferent neural activity: Neural impulses from receptors directed to the central nervous system.

Alpha (Berger) waves: EEG rhythms between about 8 and 13 Hz, most easily recordable during relaxation in a dark room and easily disrupted by light and/or mental activity.

Amplifier: A device that modifies the signals sensed, almost exclusively by increasing the signal in amplitude.

Analog: A continuous (vs. discrete) signal that may assume any value within a specified range (e.g., electrical or speech signals are analog signals).

Average evoked potential (AEP): The repetitive presentation of a stimulus produces a consistent signal that may be recorded from the scalp through signal averaging. It is thought that impulses from sensory nerves produce these slow potentials, with the primary evoked potential occurring in the sensory representation areas. Secondary average evoked potentials are recordable from any scalp location.

Baseline: In psychophysiology, usually a steady, standard, normal condition such as when the subject is in a relative state of tranquility and when a dependent variable, or set of dependent variables, is recorded prior to the administration of a special treatment. The effect of the treatment is then measured by comparison with the baseline level. The baseline is thus used to determine whether or not a reaction changed as a function of the experimental condition.

Behavior: A composite of responses where "response" is defined as activity of muscles and glands.

Behaviorism: Contemporary psychology wherein psychology is defined as the study of behavior. The typical approach is to seek lawful relationships among internal and external stimuli on the one hand, and overt and covert responses on the other hand.

Beta waves: EEG signals from about 14 to 30 Hz, thought to be present during thinking and arousal in general.

Bilabial: Referring to both lips, the term is used to describe a specific characteristic of speech. The phoneme /p/ is bilabial.

Binary: Having to do with "2." The number system with a radix (base) of two. Information may be represented in binary arithmetic as 0 or 1.

Binary coded decimal (BCD):   A number code in which individual decimal digits are each represented by a group of binary digits; in the 8-4-2-1 BCD notation, each decimal digit is represented by a four-place binary number, weighted in sequence as 8, 4, 2, and 1.

Biofeedback: Process of transducing internal bodily signals to present them to the behaver as external stimuli. In this way, the behaver can become aware of internal functioning and, in some cases, develop control over those internal systems.

Bipolar electrode placement: An electrode arrangement in which two electrodes are placed relatively close together and the changes in electrical potential between them are sensed. (Contrast with *Monopolar electrode placement.*)

Cathode ray oscilloscope (CRO):   A device containing a CRT.

Cathode ray tube (CRT):   A display device in which controlled electron beams are used to present signals on a luminescent screen.

Closed loop: A signal path in which outputs are fed back to inputs. In some circuits, there is comparison with desired values to regulate system behavior, as in servo loops.

CNS: Central nervous system consisting of the brain, spinal cord, and associated nerves.

Common-mode rejection: The ability of a differential-input circuit to discriminate against a voltage appearing at both input terminals, expressed as a ratio or log ratio.

Common-mode rejection ratio (CMRR):   Applied to differential amplifiers, a measure of the amplifier's ability to reject ambient noise such as 60 Hz interference.

Common mode voltage: A signal that appears at both terminals of a differential input device, like an amplifier.

Contingent negative variation (CNV):   A DC shift measured at the scalp that is recorded when responses to stimuli are required in a decision-making paradigm. Also called a "readiness potential" or "expectancy wave."

Covert processes: Bodily events that are not readily observable without the use of equipment or apparatus to extend the scope of our senses. The process may be behavioral (muscular or glandular) or neural (as when electroencephalographically observed). A synonym would be covert events.

Delta waves: EEG waves of less than about 4 Hz. Delta waves are abnormal in a waking adult but present at various times of sleep.

Differential amplifier: An amplifier that rejects voltages of equal amplitude and polarity that appear at both input terminals and amplifies the difference in potential between the two inputs. That potential difference is ideally the bodily signal of interest. In other words, a differential amplifier functions to reject a common-mode signal.

Efferent neural activity: Neural impulses from the brain to effectors.

Electrocardiogram: (ECG or EKG, the former anglicized, the latter from the German.) An electrical measure of heart activity consisting of a complex of signals.

Electrodermal events: An electrical measure of changes in skin potential or resistance, principally the galvanic skin response.

Electrodes: Devices for sensing electrical activity of the body. (See *Inserted electrodes,* and *Surface electrodes.*)

Electroencephalogram (EEG): An unprocessed recording of the electrical activity of the brain taken from electrodes placed on the scalp.

Electrogastrogram (EGG): Electrical records of smooth muscle activity in the abdomen.

Electromyogram (EMG): See *Muscle action potential.*

Electro-oculogram (EOG): Strictly, a recording of the slow DC shift of the standing potential between the retina and the cornea of the eye when the eye moves. More loosely, the term refers to any electrical recording of activity of the eyes.

Electropsychology: The study of psychological (behavioral) processes through electrical techniques. Traditionally the term "electro-physiology" has been used for this purpose, but "electropsychology" more appropriately refers to those small-scale bodily events that occur during cognition.

Evoked potentials (also average evoked potentials, AEP, event-related potentials, ERP): A time-locked signal (most commonly from the brain) that is revealed as a consequence of the commonality of the individual traces in a group of traces. The evoked potential is obtained by averaging a number of signals such that those events not in common are "randomized or averaged out."

Exteroceptor: A sense organ that is stimulated directly by energy changes outside the body.

Galvanic skin response: The change in the resistance of the skin to the flow of electrical current that results from changes in sweat gland activity.

Gain: In an amplifier, the ratio of output amplitude to input amplitude.

Gamma waves: EEG of about 35 to 50 Hz. This pattern is seldom encountered, and its existence is not generally accepted.

Gating: The process whereby afferent signals are controlled by efferent processes so that certain inputs are not passed to higher centers. Gating may occur while attending to one sensory modality so completely that others are excluded.

Grounding: A critical procedure that allows extraneous signals to be conducted into the ground (earth). The primary principle is to connect all metal laboratory equipment together with single leads and to direct a single lead from that system into the earth.

Hertz (Hz): Cycles per second (cps), as in 60 Hz.

Hypothetical construct: See *Mediating processes.*

Impedance: Apparent opposition to the flow of alternating current; analogous to resistance, which is the actual opposition to the flow of direct current.

Inserted electrodes: Electrodes that are placed beneath the skin of the body for sensing electrical events. Typical inserted electrodes are small needles or thin wires. (See *Electrodes,* and *Surface electrodes.*)

Integrator: An instrument that sums electrical activity over time to yield an amplitude measure. Principally used in electromyography.

Internal information processing: The interactive functioning of various systems of the body, principally neuromuscular circuits, to process externally and internally generated information.

Intervening variable: See *Mediating processes.*

Kappa waves: AN EEG rhythm of about 10 Hz found in about 30% of normal subjects, presumably evoked during problem solving.

Kymograph: A system of recording psychophysiological data that was employed during early research. The record was produced by a stylus moving on a slowly turning drum that often had been blackened by smoke.

Lingual-alveolar: Lingual refers to the tongue, and alveolar refers to the sockets of the teeth; thus the combination involves the tongue and the forward portion of the roof of the mouth. Phonemes that fall into this category include /d/, /n/, /t/, and /s/.

Linguistic response (R_L): A response that is a component of a language and is meaningful. The response may be overt as in an audible speech utterance (R_L), or it may be covert as in slight electromyographically recordable activities of the speech or nonspeech musculature (r_L).

Linguistic stimulus (S_L): Any stimulus that is a component of a language, typically a natural language, and that in some sense conveys information (such as evoking a meaning reaction).

Mediating processes: Processes that are postulated as occurring between stimulus onset and the occurrence of a response when there are lawful relations among the three events. The mediating process may be a hypothetical construct (having some physiological or psychophysiological reality) or an intervening variable (a fictitious process hypothesized merely to account for given behavior). All such mediating processes are also referred to as *logical constructs.*

Micron (μ): One millionth of a millimeter.

Microvolt (μv): One millionth of a volt (10^{-6}). The order of magnitude of the signal measured in most covert measures. Far less than the power that can be measured in the atmosphere from such radiating sources as power lines and radio stations.

Millisecond (Msec): One thousandth of a second (.001 sec).

Mind: A self-programming operation of the body that consists of, and only of, the activation of complex neuromuscular circuits. The muscular components of the circuits carry representations of stimuli that are meaningful.

Monopolar electrode placement: An arrangement of electrodes in which (typically) several electrodes are placed about the body, each of which is referred to a single common electrode. Hence, changes in electrical potential are sensed between several bodily locations and a common reference point. (Contrast with *Bipolar electrode placement.*)

Motor unit: The functional unit of skeletal muscle that consists of a nerve cell body, an axon, the terminal branches of the axon, the myoneural junction, and the muscle fibers supplied by these branches.

Muscle action potential (MAP): An electrically sensed signal that results when a localized disturbance is transmitted along a cell membrane. The disturbance then results in contraction of the fibers of the muscle. Synonymous with electromyogram. (See *Action potential*).

Muscle fiber: The structural unit of striate muscle, approximately the size of human hair.

Negative feedback: When the output signals of a system are applied to the input stage so as to modify the entire system in order to produce a stable system. Contrasted with positive feedback in which output signals are added to the input stage, increasingly driving the system so that ultimately the system goes out of control.

Neural codes: Components of the nervous systems when activated conduct neural impulses that transmit information throughout the body. The relationship between externally presented information and the neural coding in the receptor and immediately following has been extensively studied. Particularly relevant to the neuromuscular concept of internal information processing is how information is generated in the neuromuscular components.

Neuromuscular circuit: A circuit consisting of central neural components, efferent pathways, musculature components, and afferent pathways back to the central nervous system. Reverberation of these neuromuscular circuits is the essential operation in internal information processing. The processing of information received externally that is stored internally can explicate common-sense terms such as thinking and creativity. In these circuits, the musculature and brain thus interact by way of the afferent and efferent nervous pathways. Thinking is thus not just a central phenomenon, but a process that involves the entire body.

Neuromuscular junction: The surfaces where motor neurons come in contact with the musculature they innervate.

Nystagmus: An involuntary rapid movement of the eyeballs, which may be lateral, vertical, rotary, or mixed.

Occipital lobe: The posterior cortical portion of the cerebral hemisphere, which contains the main projection areas for vision.

Operational amplifier: A solid-state amplifier that employs negative feedback to improve the signal-to-noise ratio by reducing the noise within the amplifier. Hence, a signal from the output of the operational amplifier is sent back to the input so as to subtract the output voltage from the input voltage.

Orienting reflex: The complex widespread covert response pattern that alters an organism's status with respect to a stimulus.

Parietal lobe: The cortical area forward of the occipital lobes, above the temporal lobes, and posterior to the central fissure. Its function is primarily sensory.

Peripheral: A vague term referring to those portions of the body outside of the brain and spinal cord. The term causes confusion of what was traditionally referred to as the "peripheralist position" on the higher mental processes.

Peripheralism: A traditional position asserting that systems in the body other than the brain are involved in cognitive processing. Often incorrectly applied to suggest that a peripheralist doesn't ascribe cognitive functions for the brain.

Pneumogram: A breathing record of both frequency and amplitude (volume), classically accomplished by strain gauges attached to a flexible strap that is placed around the chest.

Pneumograph: A system for recording respiratory activity.

Polygraph: A common synonym for "lie detector," it is a system that includes several ink writing pens that record psychophysiological events on a slowly moving roll of paper. The pens are driven by small motors that respond to the input of any of several signals such as GSR or EEG. Because of mechnical limitations, polygraphs do not provide a linear response to input signals over 200 Hz.

Projection areas: Those areas of the brain that are primarily associated with a particular sensory modality. The occipital region is the main projection area for vision and presumably is involved in the interpretation of visual stimuli.

Proprioceptors: Those receptors that are sensitive to changes in position of portions of the body. These include receptors that signal the positions of limbs, as well as vestibular senses.

Psychophysiology: The study of those response and neural events that require laboratory apparatus for their observation. Electrical measures of psychophysiological events are the most prominent and include such covert processes as electroencephalograms, electromyograms, and electro-oculograms. For a discussion and a variety of definitions, see p. 1.

Pulse: A short-duration change in the level of a variable.

Quantification systems: In psychophysiology, those systems that render the analog signal into numerical values.

Range: The difference between the upper and lower values that can be measured.

Rapid eye movements (REM): Unique eye movements occurring during emergent Stage 1 of sleep associated with dreaming. Recording is from the external canthi for horizontal movements, and electrodes placed just above and below the eye for vertical movements.

Read: To acquire data from a source.

Read-out devices: Those systems that display and record signals.

Reference electrode: An EEG electrode placed on a subject in monopolar recording to allow potential differences to be sensed between that location (e.g., ear lobe) and a variety of others.

Sense: To detect the presence of an event.

Sensitivity: The ratio of a change in steady-state output to the corresponding change of input, often measured in percent of span.

Sensor: A device (e.g., electrode) especially and directly responsive to a measurable event.

Shielding: Placing metallic material in the environment to prevent psychophysiological signals from the body from being affected by stray fields from devices in the vicinity. (See *Shielding in,* and *Shielding out.*)

Shielding in: Confining a stray magnetic field to a limited space within a device by surrounding the device with a metallic shielding system. (See *Shielding.*)

Shielding out: Preventing stray magnetic fields from entering the laboratory (or component thereof) by placing metallic shielding material about the walls of the laboratory (or of the components).

Signal averaging: A process by which a signal is recovered from signal and noise through repeated processing of many samples that contain the signal. The noise "randomizes out," leaving only the signal, as with an average evoked potential.

Signal-to-noise ratio: A ratio that indicates the degree to which the signal dominates the noise. Ideally, we seek the largest possible signal relative to the smallest amount of noise in order to maximize the ratio.

Stimulus: Any energy that excites a receptor whereupon afferent neural impulses are generated. A stimulus may be external (outside the skin of the organism) or internal (as in neural impulses). Any stimulus results in some (overt or covert) response.

String galvanometer: An instrument that is sensitive to minute changes in current flow. Its sensitivity is a function of the low friction in the string from which the indicator is suspended, along with a coil that develops a magnetic field based on the flow of current.

Surface electrodes: Electrodes placed on the surface of the skin for sensing electrical activity. (See *Inserted electrodes,* and *Electrodes.*)

Tambour: A device, consisting of an elastic membrane, to communicate pressure changes to a recording pen.

Telemetry: A system by which a transmitter is attached to the body and transduced psychophysiological signals are sent by radio frequencies to an amplifier and a receiver.

Theta waves: EEG patterns of 4 to 7 Hz, found primarily in young children.

Transduce: To change one form of energy into another (e.g., a transducer may be employed to change electrical energy into mechanical energy so as to drive a machine with electrical signals from the body).

Adrian, E. D., & Matthews, B. H. C. The Berger rhythm: Potential changes from the occipital lobes of man. *Brain*, 1934, *57*, 355–385.

Anderson, N. H. Scales and statistics: Parametric and nonparametric. *Psychological Bulletin*, 1961, *58*, 305–316.

Arlazoroff, A., Rapoport, Y., Shanon, E., & Streifler, M. Observations on the electromyogram of the oesophagus at rest and during Valsalva's manoeuvre. *Electroencephalography and Clinical Neurophysiology*, 1972, *33*, 110–112.

Armington, J. *The electroretinogram.* New York: Academic Press, 1974.

Aserinsky, E., & Kleitman, N. Regularly occurring periods of eye motility and concomitant phenomena during sleep. *Science*, 1953, *118*, 273–274.

Aserinsky, E., & Kleitman, N. Two types of ocular motility occurring in sleep. *Journal of Applied Physiology*, 1955, *8*, 1–10.

Ax, A. F. Editorial. *Psychophysiology*, 1964, *1*, 1–3.

Basmajian, J. V. *Muscles alive: Their functions revealed by electromyography.* Baltimore: Williams & Wilkins, 1962.

Basmajian, J. R., Baeza, M., & Fabrigar, C. Conscious control and training of individual spinal motor neurons in normal human subjects. *Journal of New Drugs*, 1965, *5*, 78–85.

Bechterev, V. M. *Foundations of general reflexology of man.* Moscow: Gosizdat, 1923.

Berger, H. Über das elektrenkephalogramm des Menschen. *Archiv fur Psychiatrie Nervenkrankheiten*, 1929, *87*, 527–570.

Black, H. S. Stabilized feedback amplifiers. *Bell System Tech. Journal*, 1934, *13*, 1–18.

Boneau, C. A. The effects of violations of assumptions underlying the *t* test. *Psychological Bulletin*, 1960, *57*, 49–64.

Box, G. E. P. Some theories on quadratic forms applied in the study of analysis of variance problems: II. Effects of inequality of variance and covariance between errors in the two-way classification. *Annals of Mathematical Statistics*, 1954, *25*, 484–498.

Bradley, J. V. *Studies in research methodology VI. The Central limit effect for a variety of populations and the robustness of Z, t, and F.* AMRL Technical Documentary Report 64-123, 6570th Aerospace Medical Research Laboratories, Wright-Patterson Air Force Base, Ohio, December, 1964.

Brown, M. W., Edge, G. M., & Horn, G. A miniature transmitter suitable for telemetry of a wide range of biopotentials. *Electroencephalography and Clinical Neurophysiology*, 1971, *31*, 274–276.

Brown, P. B., Maxfield, B. W., & Moraff, H. *Electronics for neurobiologists.* Cambridge, Mass.: MIT Press, 1973.

Brumlik, J., Richeson, W. B., & Arbit, J. The origin of certain electrical cerebral rhythms. *Brain Research*, 1966/1967, *3*, 227–247.

Caceres, C. A., & Cooper, J. K. Telemetry in medicine and biology. In S. N. Levine (Ed.), *Advances in biomedical engineering and medical physics* (Vol. 1). New York: Wiley, 1968.

Camishion, R. C. *Basic medical electronics.* Boston, Mass.: Little, Brown & Co., 1964.

Chase, W. G. (Ed.). *Visual information processing.* New York: Academic Press, 1973.

Cohen, H. L., & Brumlik, J. *A manual of electroneuromyography.* New York: Harper, 1968.

Cohen, J. Very slow brain potentials relating to expectancy: The CNV. In E. Donchin & D. B. Lindsley (Eds.), *Average evoked potentials.* Washington, D.C.: NASA SP-191, 1969.

Darrow, C. W. Psychophysiology, yesterday, today, and tomorrow. *Psychophysiology,* 1964, *1,* 4–7.

Davis, J. F. *Manual of surface electromyography* (WADC Tech. Rep. 59–184). Ohio: Wright Air Development Center, December 1959.

Davis, R. C. The relations of certain muscle action potentials during "Mental Work." *Indiana University Publication Science Series,* 1937, *5,* 29.

Davis, R. C., Garafolo, L., & Gault, F. P. An exploration of abdominal potentials. *Journal of Comparative and Physiological Psychology,* 1957, *50,* 519–523.

Davis, R. C., Garafolo, L., & Kveim, K. Conditions associated with gastrointestinal activity. *Journal of Comparative and Physiological Psychology,* 1959, *52,* 466–475.

Dawson, W. W., & Doddington, H. W. *Extraction of signal from noise without phase error.* Unpublished manuscript, University of Florida, Gainesville, Fla.

Delafresnaye, J. F. *Brain mechanisms and consciousness.* Springfield, Ill.: Charles C. Thomas, 1954.

Donchin, E. Data analysis techniques in average evoked potential research. In E. Donchin & D. B. Lindsley (Eds.), *Average evoked potentials.* Washington, D.C.: NASA SP-191, 1969.

duBois-Reymond, E. Untersuchungen über thierische Electricität. *Berlin, G. Reimer,* 1849, *2,* 256.

Dunlap, K. *A system of psychology.* New York: Scribner's, 1912.

Eccles, J. C. *The neurophysiological basis of mind.* London: Oxford University Press, 1953.

Eccles, J. C. *Brain and conscious experience.* New York: Springer-Verlag, 1966.

Edwards, A. L. *Experimental design in psychological research* (1st ed.). New York: Holt, Rinehart & Winston, 1950.

Ellingson, R. J. Brain waves and problems of psychology. *Psychological Bulletin,* 1956, *53,* 1–34.

Faaborg-Andersen, K., & Edfeldt, A. W. Electromyography of intrinsic and extrinsic laryngeal muscles during silent speech: Correlation with reading activity. *Acta oto-laryngologica,* 1958, *49,* 478–482.

Fleming, D. G., & Feinberg, B. N. *Handbook of engineering in medicine and biology.* Cleveland, Ohio: CRC Press, 1975.

Fogel, L. J., & George, F. W. *Progress in biomedical engineering.* Washington, D.C.: Spartan Books, 1967.

Fox, S. S., & Rosenfeld, J. P. Recording evoked potentials. In R. D. Myers (Ed.), *Methods in psychobiology. Volume 2. Specialized techniques in neuropsychology and neurobiology.* New York: Academic Press, 1973.

Galperin, P. Y. Stages in the development of mental acts. In M. Cole & I. Maltzman (Eds.), *A handbook of contemporary Soviet psychology.* New York: Basic Books, 1969.

Gatev, V., & Ivanov, I. Excitation–contraction latency in human muscles. *Agressologie*, 1972, *13*, 7–12.

Geddes, L. A. *Electrodes and the measurement of bioelectric events.* New York: Wiley-Interscience, 1972.

Geddes, L. A., & Baker, L. E. *Principles of applied biomedical instrumentation.* New York: Wiley, 1968.

Goff, W. R., Matsumiya, Y., Allison, T., & Goff, G. D. Cross-modality comparisons of average evoked potentials. In E. Donchin & D. B. Lindsley (Eds.), *Average evoked potentials.* Washington, D.C.: NASA SP-191, 1969.

Goldwater, B. C. Psychological significance of pupillary movements. *Psychological Bulletin,* 1972, *77,* 340–355.

Greenfield, N. S., & Sternback, R. A. (Eds.). *Handbook of psychophysiology.* New York: Holt, Rinehart & Winston, 1972.

Grings, W. W. *Laboratory instrumentation in psychology.* Palo Alto, Calif.: National Press, 1954.

Grings, W. W. The role of consciousness and cognition in autonomic behavior change. In F. J. McGuigan & R. A. Schoonover (Eds.), *The psychophysiology of thinking.* New York: Academic Press, 1973. (a)

Grings, W. W. Cognitive factors in electrodermal conditioning. *Psychological Bulletin,* 1973, *79,* 200–210. (b)

Guld, C., Rosenfalck, A., & Willison, R. G. Report of the committee on EMG instrumentation. Technical factors in recording electrical activity of muscle and nerve in man. *Electroencephalography and Clinical Neurophysiology,* 1970, *28,* 299–413.

Hanley, J., Adey, W. R., Zweizig, J. R., & Kado, R. T. EEG electrode-amplifier harness. *Electroencephalography and Clinical Neurophysiology,* 1971, *30,* 147–150.

Hebb, D. O. *The organization of behavior.* New York: Wiley, 1949.

Hebb, D. O. Concerning imagery. *Psychological Review,* 1968, *75,* 466–477.

Hefferline, R. F., Keenan, B., Harford, R. A., & Birch, J. Electronics in psychology. *Columbia Engineering Quarterly,* 1960, *13,* 10–15.

Hernández-Peón, R., Scherrer, H., & Jouvet, M. Modification of electric activity in cochlear nucleus during "attention" in unanaesthetized cats. *Science,* 1956, *123,* 331–332.

Hill, J. D., & Parr, G. (Eds.). *Electroencephalography: A symposium on its various aspects.* London: MacDonald, 1963.

Hirano, M., & Ohala, J. Use of hooked-wire electrodes for electromyography of the intrinsic laryngeal muscles. *Journal of Speech and Hearing Research,* 1969, *12,* 362–373.

Hixon, T. J., Tiebens, A. A., & Minifie, F. D. An EMG electrode for the diaphragm. *Journal of the Acoustical Society of America,* 1969, *46,* 1588–1596.

Holt, E. B. Materialism and the criterion of the psychic. *Psychological Review,* 1937, *44,* 33–53.

Hull, C. L. *Principles of behavior.* New York: Appleton-Century-Crofts, 1943.

Hunter, W. S. The problem of consciousness. *Psychological Review,* 1924, *31,* 1–37.

Jackson, H. W. *Introduction to electrical circuits* (4th ed.). Englewood Cliffs, N.J.: Prentice-Hall, 1975.

Jacobson, E. Voluntary relaxation of the esophagus. *American Journal of Physiology,* 1925, *72,* 387–394.

Jacobson, E. Action currents from muscular contractions during conscious processes. *Science,* 1927, *66,* 403.

Jacobson, E. *Progressive relaxation.* Chicago: University of Chicago Press, 1929.

Jacobson, E. Electrical measurements of neuromuscular states during mental activities. III. Visual imagination and recollection. *American Journal of Physiology,* 1930, *95,* 694–702.

Jacobson, E. Electrophysiology of mental activities. *American Journal of Psychology,* 1932, *44,* 677–694.

Jacobson, E. *Progressive relaxation* (rev. ed.). Chicago: University of Chicago Press, 1938. (a)

Jacobson, E. *You can sleep well.* New York: McGraw-Hill, 1938. (b)

Jacobson, E. Electrophysiology of mental activities and introduction to the psychological process of thinking. In F. J. McGuigan & R. A. Schoonover (Eds.), *The psychophysiology of thinking.* New York: Academic Press, 1973.

Johnson, J. B., & Murphree, O. D. Direct-current fluorescent lighting for experimental chambers. *Psychophysiology,* 1972, *9,* 663–664.

Karlin, L. Cognition, preparation, and sensory-evoked potentials. *Psychological Bulletin,* 1970, *73,* 122–136.

Kiang, N. *Discharge patterns of single fibers in the cat's auditory nerve.* Cambridge, Mass.: MIT Press, 1966.

Kimmich, H. P., & Vos, J. A. (Eds.). *Biotelemetry. International Symposium.* Leiden, Netherlands: Meander, 1972.

Kleitman, N. Patterns of dreaming. *Scientific American,* 1960, *203,* 82–103.

Kolta, P. Strong and permanent interaction between peripheral nerve and a constant inhomogeneous magnetic field. *Acta Physiologica Academiae Scientiarum Hungaricae,* 1973, *43,* 89–94.

Kris, C. Vision: Electro-oculography. In O. Glasser (Ed.), *Medical physics.* Chicago: The Yearbook Publishers, 1960.

Lacey, B. C., & Lacey, J. I. Studies of heart rate and other bodily processes in sensorimotor behavior. In P. A. Obrist, A. H. Black, J. Brener, & L. V. DiCara (Eds.), *Cardiovascular psychophysiology: Current issues in response mechanism, biofeedback, and methodology.* Chicago: Aldine-Atherton, 1974.

Lacey, J. I. Individual differences in somatic response patterns. *Journal of Comparative and Physiological Psychology,* 1950, *43,* 338–350.

Ladefoged, P. Sub-glottal activity during speech. *Proceedings of the Fourth International Congress of Phonetic Sciences, Helsinki, 1961.* The Hague: Mouton, 1962.

Langfeld, H. S. A response interpretation of consciousness. *Psychological Review,* 1931, *38,* 87–108.

Langfeld, H. S. The historical development of response psychology. *Science,* 1933, *77,* 243–250.

Leontiev, A. N. *Problems of psychic development.* Moscow: APN RSFSR Press, 1959.

Levine, S. N. (Ed.). *Advances in biomedical engineering and medical physics.* New York: Wiley-Interscience, 1968.

Lindquist, E. F. *Design and analysis of experiments in psychology and education* (1st ed.). Boston: Houghton Mifflin, 1953.

Lindsay, P. H., & Norman, D. A. *Human information processing. An introduction to psychology.* New York: Academic Press, 1972.

Lindsey, J. W. The auditory evoked potential in man: A review. *T. -I. -T. Journal of Life Sciences,* 1971, *1,* 91–110.

Lindsley, D. B. Electroencephalography. In J. McV. Hunt (Ed.), *Personality and the behavior disorders* (Vol. 2). New York: Ronald Press, 1944.

Lindsley, D. B. Average evoked potentials—Achievements, failures and prospects. In E. Donchin & D. B. Lindsley (Eds.), *Average evoked potentials.* Washington, D. C.: NASA SP-191, 1969.

Lippold, O. Origin of the alpha rhythm. *Nature,* 1970, *226,* 616–618. (a)

Lippold, O. Bilateral separation in alpha rhythm recording. *Nature,* 1970, *226,* 459–460. (b)

Lippold, O. Are alpha waves artefactual? *New Scientist,* 1970, March 12, 506–507. (c)

Lippold, O. C. J., & Novotny, G. E. K. Is alpha rhythm an artefact? *Lancet,* 1970, *1,* 976–979.

Lockhart, R. D., & Brandt, W. Length of striated muscle fibres. *Journal of Anatomy,* 1937–1938, *72.*

Lykken, D. T., Rose, R., Luther, B., & Maley, M. Correcting psychophysiological measures for individual differences in range. *Psychological Bulletin,* 1966, *66,* 481–484.

MacCorquodale, K., & Meehl, P. E. On a distinction between hypothetical constructs and intervening variables. *Psychological Review,* 1948, *55,* 95–107.

Mackay, R. S. *Bio-medical telemetry* (2nd ed.). New York: Wiley, 1970.

Malmstadt, H. V., Enke, C. G., & Toren, E. C., Jr. *Electronics for scientists. Principles and experiments for those who use instruments.* New York: W. A. Benjamin, 1963.

Marg, E. Development of electro-oculography. *A.M.A. Archives of Ophthalmology,* 1951, *45,* 169–185.

Max, L. W. An experimental study of the motor theory of consciousness. III. Action–current responses in deaf mutes during sleep, sensory stimulation and dreams. *Journal of Comparative Psychology,* 1935, *19,* 469–486.

Max, L. W. An experimental study of the motor theory of consciousness. IV. Action–current responses in the deaf during awakening, kinaesthetic imagery and abstract thinking. *Journal of Comparative Psychology,* 1937, *24,* 301–344.

McGuigan, F. J. Covert oral behavior and auditory hallucinations. *Psychophysiology,* 1966, *3,* 73–80.

McGuigan, F. J. Covert oral behavior as a function of quality of handwriting. *American Journal of Psychology,* 1970, *83,* 377–388.

McGuigan, F. J. Covert linguistic behavior in deaf subjects during thinking. *Journal of Comparative and Physiological Psychology,* 1971, *75,* 417–420.

McGuigan, F. J. Conditioning of covert behavior: Some problems and some hopes. In F. J. McGuigan & D. B. Lumsden (Eds.), *Contemporary approaches to conditioning and learning.* Washington, D.C.: V. H. Winston, 1973.

McGuigan, F. J. *Cognitive psychophysiology: Principles of covert behavior.* Englewood Cliffs, N.J.: Prentice-Hall, 1978.

McGuigan, F. J., & Boness, D. J. What happens between an external stimulus and an overt response? A study of covert responses. *Pavlovian Journal of Biological Science*, 1975, *10*, 112–119.

McGuigan, F. J., Culver, V. I., & Kendler, T. S. Covert behavior as a direct electromyographic measure of mediating responses. *Conditional Reflex*, 1971, *6*, 145–152.

McGuigan, F. J., Keller, B., & Stanton, E. Covert language responses during silent reading. *Journal of Educational Psychology*, 1964, *55*, 339–343.

McGuigan, F. J., & Pavek, G. V. On the psychophysiological identification of covert nonoral language processes. *Journal of Experimental Psychology*, 1972, *92*, 237–245.

McGuigan, F. J., & Pinkney, K. B. Effects of increased reading rate on covert processes. *Interamerican Journal of Psychology*, 1973, *7*, 223–231.

McGuigan, F. J., & Winstead, C. L., Jr. Discriminative relationship between covert oral behavior and the phonemic system in internal information processing. *Journal of Experimental Psychology*, 1974, *103*, 885–890.

Mowrer, O. H., Ruch, T. C., & Miller, N. E. The corneo–retinal potential differences as the basis of the galvanometric method of recording eye movements. *American Journal of Physiology*, 1936, *114*, 423–428.

Myers, R. D. (Ed.). *Methods in psychobiology. Volume 2. Specialized techniques in neuropsychology and neurobiology.* New York: Academic Press, 1973.

Northrop, F. S. C. *The logic of the sciences and the humanities.* New York: Macmillan, 1948.

Offner, F. F. *Electronics for biologists.* New York: McGraw-Hill, 1967.

Osgood, C. E., & Hoosain, R. Salience of the word as a unit in the perception of language. *Perception and Psychophysics*, 1974, *15*, 168–192.

Pavlov, I. P. *Lectures on conditioned reflexes. Volume II. Conditioned reflexes and psychiatry.* New York: International Publishers, 1941.

Penfield, W. Consciousness, memory, and man's conditioned reflexes. In K. H. Pribram (Ed.), *On the biology of learning.* New York: Harcourt Brace Jovanovich, 1969.

Peters, J. F. Eye movement recording: A brief review. *Psychophysiology*, 1971, *8*, 414–415.

Razran, G. H. S. A quantitative study of meaning by a conditioned salivary technique (semantic conditioning). *Science*, 1939, *90*, 89–90.

Regan, D. *Evoked potentials in psychology, sensory physiology and clinical medicine.* London: Chapman & Hall, 1972.

Reichenbach, H. *Atom and cosmos.* London: Allen & Unwin, 1932.

Schmitt, F. O. (Ed.-in-Chief). *The neurosciences: Second study program.* New York: Rockefeller University Press, 1970.

Sechenov, I. M. *Reflexes of the brain.* In I. M. Sechenov, *Selected works.* Moscow and Leningrad: State Publishing House for Biological and Medical Literature, 1935. [Originally published in St. Petersburg, 1863. In R. J. Herrnstein & E. G. Boring (Eds.), *A source book in the history of psychology.* Cambridge, Mass.: Harvard University Press, 1965.]

Shackel, B. Eye movement recording by electro-oculography. In P. H. Venables & I. Martin, *A manual of psychophysiological methods.* Amsterdam: North-Holland, 1967.

Shagass, C. *Evoked brain potentials in psychiatry.* New York: Plenum Press, 1972.

Sheatz, G. C. A differential microvolt test signal adjustable to given laboratory requirements. *Psychophysiology,* 1972, *9,* 658–659.

Sidowski, J. B. *Experimental methods and instrumentation in psychology.* New York: McGraw-Hill, 1966.

Smith, C. U. M. *The brain: Toward an understanding.* New York: Putnam's, 1970.

Smith, M. O. History of the motor theories of attention. *Journal of General Psychology,* 1969, *80,* 243–257.

Snedecor, G. W. *Statistical methods* (4th ed.). Ames, Iowa: Iowa State College Press, 1946.

Society Proceedings of the American Electroencephalographic Society, Bloomington, Minnesota, September 16–18, 1971. *Electroencephalography and Clinical Neurophysiology,* 1972, *33,* 237–255.

Stern, J. A. Toward a definition of psychophysiology. *Psychophysiology,* 1964, *1,* 90–91.

Suprynowicz, V. A. *Introduction to electronics for students of biology, chemistry, and medicine.* Reading, Mass.: Addison-Wesley, 1966.

Sutton, S. The specification of psychological variables in an average evoked potential experiment. In E. Donchin & D. B. Lindsley (Eds.), *Average evoked potentials.* Washington, D.C.: NASA SP-191, 1969.

Tecce, J. J. Contingent negative variation and individual differences: A new approach in brain research. *Archives of General Psychiatry,* 1971, *24,* 1–16.

Tecce, J. J. Contingent negative variation (CNV) and psychological processes in man. *Psychological Bulletin,* 1972, *77,* 73–108.

Thompson, R. F., & Patterson, M. M. (Eds.). *Bioelectric recording techniques.* New York: Academic Press 1973, 1974. (A three-volume treatise, Parts A, B, & C.)

Thorson, A. M. The relation of tongue movements to internal speech. *Journal of Experimental Psychology,* 1925, *8,* 1–32.

Titchener, E. B. *Lectures on the experimental psychology of the thought processes.* New York: Macmillan, 1909.

Tocci, R. J. *Fundamentals of electronic devices* (2nd ed.). Columbus, Ohio: Bobbs-Merrill, 1975.

Tolman, E. C. *Purposive behavior in animals and men.* New York: Appleton-Century-Crofts, 1932.

Tukey, J. W. One degree of freedom for nonadditivity. *Biometrics,* 1949, *5,* 232–242.

Tursky, B., & O'Connell, D. N. A comparison for AC and DC eye movement recording. *Psychophysiology,* 1966, *3,* 157–163.

Vaughan, H. G., Jr. The relationship of brain activity to scalp recordings of event-related potentials. In E. Donchin & D. B. Lindsley (Eds.), *Average evoked potentials.* Washington, D.C.: NASA SP-191, 1969.

Venables, P. H., & Martin, I. (Eds.). *A manual of psychophysiological methods.* Amsterdam: North-Holland, 1967.

Vigotsky, L. S. *Thought and language.* New York: Wiley, 1962.

Watson, J. B. *Behavior: An introduction to comparative psychology.* New York: Holt, 1914.

Watson, J. B. *Behaviorism* (rev. ed.). Chicago: University of Chicago Press, 1930.

Wilkinson, R. T., Herbert, M., & Branton, P. A "pocket" portable EEG recorder: Adapting the Stott Miniature Analog Tape Recording System to record sleeping EEG on trains. *APSS San Diego,* 1973.

Winer, B. J. *Statistical principles in experimental design* (2nd ed.). New York: McGraw-Hill, 1971.

Yanof, H. M. *Biomedical electronics* (2nd ed.). Philadelphia: F. A. Davis Co., 1973.

Young, R. M. *Mind, brain and adaptation in the nineteenth century.* New York: Oxford University Press, 1970.

Young, L. R., & Sheena, D. Eye-movement measurement techniques. *American Psychologist,* 1975, *30,* 315–330.

Zimmer, H., & Krusberg, R. J. *Psychophysiologic components of human behavior: A compendium.* Athens, Ga.: University of Georgia Press, 1966.

AUTHOR INDEX

Italic numbers denote pages with bibliographic information.

SUBJECT INDEX